The Best-Selling Author of
Getting to "I Do" and *Staying Married and Loving It*

Patricia Allen, PhD

IT'S A MAN'S WORLD AND A WOMAN'S UNIVERSE

PATRICIA ALLEN, PHD.

ORIGINAL COVER PAINTING BY
FRAN ESTAVILLO COMSTOCK

BALBOA.
PRESS
A DIVISION OF HAY HOUSE

Balboa Press books may be ordered through booksellers or by contacting:

Balboa Press
A Division of Hay House
1663 Liberty Drive
Bloomington, IN 47403
www.balboapress.com
1 (877) 407-4847

Print information available on the last page.

ISBN: 978-1-5043-7007-3 (sc)
ISBN: 978-1-5043-7009-7 (hc)
ISBN: 978-1-5043-7008-0 (e)

Library of Congress Control Number: 2016921114

Balboa Press rev. date: 02/03/2017

ACKNOWLEDGMENTS

I wish to thank Jennifer Jan Jones, a gifted writer, philosopher, and teacher, for her contributions to the "Holy Grail" aspects of this book. To my daughter, Sue Wagner, thank you for guiding this book into print! Thank you, Betzi Richardson, for the poetry of words you helped create. To Andy Shaw, thank you for the manuscript editing and technical preparation. To Ed Rapka, I want to say thank you for editing *Conversational Rape* (Allen). Lastly, thank you, H.P., for the inspiration I needed to write this book.

CONTENTS

FOREWORD

It has been years since *Getting to "I Do"* was published. Much has happened, and much has been learned. I am so very grateful that so many women and men have gotten into loving relationships, married, or mated—which is not legally married but sexually and socially monogamous, continuous, and definitely long-term, using the information I compiled. But what about those who fell into the cracks of relationships or marital failure? How did that happen, and what should be the response?

In the old days, men were men and women were women, but this is no longer true. Today we have multiple choices, and we need new concepts if we are to mate and marry. Due to poor role modeling by divorced parents and conflicting media images of maleness (yang) and femaleness (yin), men and women are creating a mixture of old traditions and new-age values to the confusion of everyone.

Western culture has traditionally cast the male gender as protectors, leaders, providers of *things*, and doers. Men have traditionally proposed to women, have conferred status upon women, and have supplied financial security. Women have been the domesticators of children, the followers of men, and the grateful recipients of *things*. Men have made their plans for women and children, and women have responded sensually and sexually.

Men controlled things, and patriarchs ruled pragmatically. In those days, churches, ethnic groups, and cultures ordered men and women to behave in certain ways. Men were supposed to give to, protect, and cherish women and children. Women were expected to passively wait to receive respectfully and respond sensually by homemaking and sexuality. Unmarried women either stayed home with mom and dad or supported themselves in low-paying jobs.

In the early 1970's, the feminist movement burst on the scene. For the first time, women could actively pursue maleness (yang), male qualities that represented success. Money, power, independence, and prestige were all within a woman's grasp, and for the first time in the western world they could be realistically achieved by women without sacrificing cultural values.

Instead, traditional female roles were sacrificed, that for generations had been the loving foundation of relationships, the life beneath, the *air*, the universe. Women were often ashamed of being satisfied with the traditional female role. In reaction, men picked up the female, passive, receptive roles, and marriages declined as a result. Women—not men—initiated divorces in the first three years of marriage, as they were dissatisfied by the loss of equality and independence through motherhood. Men saw value in sharing responsibilities, especially financial ones, with hardworking "supermom" women.

Soon there were no rules of behavior except the matriarchal rules imposed by strong women on men. She could call him, and she could initiate sex. In courting and dating, equality became the name of the game. He fought for his opinions, and she fought for hers. He wanted his feelings taken care of, and so did she. The problem was that instead of two people in a graceful waltz of give and take, marriage and dating became a kind of battleground on which men and women sought equal status and equal degrees of power and prestige.

With both men and women vying for the same position, the dance was abandoned as two partners struggled for the lead. In the process, we lost the skills of making love to one another.

This three-part book—*I-ness* dealing with individuality, *we-ness* dealing with the couple (gay, straight, or lesbian), and *us-ness* dealing with the couple in a world of friends, families, stepfamilies, ex-families, work, and extramarital relationships—is a spiritual study of how to love one another in today's "equal," narcissistically-oriented world of money, power, and prestige.

I still have two offices, one in Newport Beach and one in L.A. I have my two seminars weekly as well as fun chances to carry my message on TV and radio and even a movie, *Duty Dating*, created by a client, Cherry Norris. (She gave permission to disclose her name.)

This book is especially dedicated to the confused men who don't know how to deal with today's liberated but tired, frustrated single moms, single-forever, multi-married, independent women, and to all you liberated women who are tired of passive-aggressive, non-committable, commitment-phobic or noncommittal, or committing men who look to you to lead them, give to them, cherish them, and mother them *first* before you receive and give back.

My promise to both men and women is that after applying the information you learn from reading this book you will have gained great insight.

Men will:

1. Learn that some women don't know how to be spiritual muses and that you must teach them your needs even when it's painful.
2. Not fall into the sexual trap. There are *no* free lunches or lays.
3. Have the communication skills to negotiate with any woman you may want to mate with or legally marry.

Women will:

1. Learn how to spot the difference between a creative, feminine anima "monk" man and a using, abusing momma's boy *Peter Pan*. A creative anima-based monk may not have made it financially, but he never uses or abuses his woman. He may be an actor, musician, writer, artist, teacher, nurse, or minister. He is still a respectable man when it comes to cherishing a woman who respects him.
2. Not allow your sexual nature as a receptive woman to override your common sense by having premature intercourse and bonding you to a man you hardly know.
3. Develop the communication skills to negotiate with any man, spiritual or not, whether you want a legal marriage and family or a non-documented, long-term, sexually and socially monogamous and continuous (at least once a week) relationship.

INTRODUCTION

The title *It's a Man's World and a Woman's Universe* creatively pulled on me even before I wrote *Getting to 'I Do'*. William Morrow Publishing chose *Getting to 'I Do'* and I believe that was the appropriate title for it. That book was aimed at women getting married. It was not particularly directed toward men and their issues, though this book is.

The second book, *Staying Married and Loving It*, was directed toward people in relationships, married, or mated, and how to communicate, especially in times of conflict. This three-part book is meant to deal with the games that occur when a couple thinks they are "doing it the Pat Allen way," and it still fails.

These three books within one book also attempt to delve into the spiritual love needs of good men and women—people who pride themselves on their personal integrity and virtue. As I always say, the only way you know you love yourself or anyone else, is by the commitments you are willing to make and keep.

"It's a man's world" refers to yang energy, not gender. Some of today's women are more yang men than yin women. These women are assertive, smart, decisive, proactive, independent, upwardly-mobile, career-oriented, and also health-conscious; they are clothes-smart, body-building, and they rebuild with plastic surgery—yang masculine active energy. The pragmatic goals of yang energy men and women are money, power, and prestige in this world.

The acquisition of things, the use of things, and the control over things brings gratification. To *do good* is to *feel good* about oneself. To be respected is most important.

"It's a woman's universe" refers to yin energy, also not to gender. Some of today's men are more feminine than many women. They are more receptive to being given to, want to be cherished for their feelings, and are available to assertive women who want them. They are more respecting of women's rights to lead, decide, and take charge. Yin feminine energy can also be expressed by either men or women.

The goal of yin-energy men and women is the universal ethereal *air* of relationships at home and at work. Yin men and women control the oxygen of communication. They have the veto right to say no to negotiating mutually beneficial agreements. They can turn off the air by playing communication games of intimidation through fear and/or games of seduction through guilt and shame. To *feel good* is to *do good* in relationships and in life. To be cherished is of the greatest importance.

This book will answer the following questions:

1. Why do women change after the wedding or commitment?
2. Why do men want things to stay the same after the wedding or commitment?
3. How can you tell if she or he has personal integrity and virtue?
4. Why can't equality work?
5. Is spirituality different from religion?
6. Why does it take a year to know someone?
7. Can *love* carry a relationship successfully? Or does it take hard negotiations for right actions?
8. Why does a "friendship" not advance past the first lay?
9. Why are more men so interested in yang energy women (money, power, and prestige)?
10. Why are more women interested in yin energy men (physicality, feelings, and relationships)?
11. What is the difference between power games of intimidation and seduction and potent loving through negotiation of *wants* and *not wants*?
12. Can you trust a human being before you know him or her?

1

THE GLOBAL WOUNDS OF THE FISHER KING, PAST AND PRESENT

Today's religious wars in the Middle East remind me of when the grail legends first appeared in Europe. The entire continent was in turmoil. On the surface, there were pilgrimages and free access to many cultures, but the only established central authority was the Church of Rome.

Today, Islam holds that position in the Middle East. Kingdoms then were bickering over (and conquering and coveting) land, as are tribal areas today, and emphasis on any other kind of secular equivalent was not—and still is not—a priority. Saddam Hussein and Osama bin Laden were the latest religious-secular leaders, much like the Roman popes of yesterday.

During the Crusades, persecution was aimed at all those who did not bow to the letter of the Roman Church's dogma and invariably included the most innovative minds of the age and, predictably, the spawn of Eve. The big campaign during the eleventh and twelfth centuries was, of course, the Crusades. It has been estimated that the Crusades cost about ten million innocent lives.

Today's campaign, including September 11, 2001, is international terrorism in the name of God. Both religious systems, past and present, reacted to what they declared as heresy with an increasingly fanatical and dictatorial zeal, virtually unhindered in their purges through bombings and biochemical annihilation of innocents.

Science and the female principle of yin, and loving relationships disappeared out of sight then and now. Our spiritual evolution also disappeared with these losses.

The two major wounds, then in Europe, and today and yesterday in the Far East (today's Middle East) are still bleeding. These wounds are the following:

1. The repression of women (as in Afghanistan); the yin, female principle of feeling-centeredness, physical security, and safe nurturing; and the feminine principle of the right of each human being to receive agape love exemplified by the concepts of *I wish you well* and *Do unto others as you would have them do unto you.*
2. The creation of the wastelands of war zones and the wounding of the individual self.

2

MYTH SPEAKS THE LANGUAGE OF ETERNAL RETURNS, CYCLES RENEWED, AND HEROES REBORN

The archetypal elements of the Arthurian Grail and the bleeding lance are the classic sexual symbols for the masculine yang and feminine yin principles. It is only when these two are united that the wasteland of war (the barren realm of the Grail castle of the Earth) can be restored. This is the wound that must be healed before there can be a return to paradise in both a global and individual sense. The quest for the Grail can also be interpreted in psychological terms as the return of the son to the mother.

In the Parzival scenario, the hero leaves his mother to join the knights, despite her fear that he will die—as her brothers and father did before him in the mongerings of war. He leaves the figurative womb of his mother when he follows the knights from the wilderness.

In other words, every baby is a hero passing through psychological as well as physical transformation from a water creature (in an amniotic paradise) to an air-breathing mammal (reflected in the age of Aquarius) that has to face a dangerous unknown without boundaries. With his egocentric drive, he doesn't notice his mother's death as he leaves the childhood paradise. He is intoxicated with the birth of independence, a new existence, and a sense of freedom.

In many versions, it is his sin that first prevents him from curing the Fisher King wound by failing to ask the question "What ails thee, Uncle?" In his excitement of attainment, he has failed to keep within him the nurturing caretaker of the feminine principle.

This also prevents him from healing the earth of its wounds (the wasteland of bombings, war, violence, and rape of resources) by not

3

cherishing the internal yin soul and what was given to humankind to enjoy and share.

When he leaves his own queen, it is to seek his mother, but he finds the Grail instead. He cannot return to the womb of his mother, so he must find the internal mother of the universe within him—his soul, his yin energy, his anima—the castle in which the hero is invisible to all but the worthy (with water being a metaphor for womb and spirituality). This can be seen as the womb of the new mother who is now rediscovered by her son/lover inasmuch as every lover/yin is a son and every mistress/yang is a mother.

Sexuality and sensuality lead to an internal power that bodes castration to the power of religion, then and now. Cover yourself; hide away, and be quiet. Passion, even in its academic sense—or as motivation for advancement of the human condition—was and is today greatly feared in the Middle East, for it knows no boundaries, no rules of order. It is pure, passionate emotion in laser focus.

The patriarchs jeered at it and called it obsessive, but the troubadours and all the Romantic poets who revered its power loved it. William Blake spoke of obsession as being the doorway to wisdom, which led Jim Morrison to name his band The Doors.

E-motion (energy's motion)

The brain is set up to chemically reward each new insight, revelation, epiphany, and creative expression. We are genetically engineered to be motivated to not just preserve the species, but also to help it evolve. To deny passionate emotion's chemical value is to diminish our potential for progress. Jesus said, "If you bring forth what is within you, what you bring forth will save you. If you do not bring forth what is within you, what you do not bring forth will destroy you". (Gospel of Thomas)

Then and now in the Middle East, religion teaches that passion is something to be feared, controlled, and regulated in the service of power. As in all things, passion has its duality.

The passions of hate and bigotry in the name of religion run rampant against science, art, sexuality, and sensuality—yet we are told we must still control our passions, our evil urges, and our need to question God's will.

The wrath of Jehovah is instilled against those who would eat of the tree of knowledge lest they "become like one of us" (Gen. 3:22) and fearful Zeuses of Mount Olympus threaten to punish each new Prometheus for bringing fire to man.

They would not have any of the masses climb to higher altitudes to claim residence in or infiltrate their ivory towers. The elements of power are always opposed to change and new perspective because these remove them from their seat of control. The enemy of the power currently in control in the Middle East will always be the power with the potential to unseat it from its throne. "The players tried to take the field, but the marching band refused to yield." (Don McLean, "American Pie").

Our martyrs of sacred passion—men of good will—will now have little bearing, save temporary restitution, because fear and greed have enslaved many of us of the world, and we are willing to surrender. Our lessons of love, the feminine yin principle of energy, from all the great teachers and philosophers, are falling fallow, because too many men long for what they do not have and substitute things (yang) for what they cannot passionately find.

Betwixt and between passion and love for love's sake of the flower-children generation lies a different path.

For sake for sake and for own sake.

At the crossroads of passion and love is not the sacrifice of martyrs; it is not the passion of egocentric gratification. It does not deny the self but instead enhances the self through purpose of a higher order. It answers the futile swing of the pendulum's paradox back and forth from yin to yang repeatedly. It is the mystical kingdom between the two mountains. It is the ravine within its valley, ready to be filled with living waters of a new perception.

And like Parzival, we must pierce this valley of the unknown and risk letting go in order to rise to the next level.

To do so academically in a yang way will never be enough. To quest in theory or in unbalanced measure of falsehood cannot unlock the higher frequency that will transcend us chemically (with yin feelings) and electrically (through yang thoughts). Both yin and yang must be used simultaneously to unlock the spiritual secrets of the Grail.

3

FORGET WHAT YOU KNOW, AND REMEMBER WHAT YOU HAVE FORGOTTEN

At virtually every point of the hero's quest, he finds a female guide, a muse, or a signpost. This is almost like a chess game, in which the opposing king can only be checked with the cooperation of the queen, who can assume the shape of all the other pieces on the chessboard except the knights.

The queen appears in many forms: a teacher, a minister or nun, a therapist, a doctor, a lawyer, a neighbor, or a relative. She is the only piece that can move (or speak) as far as she likes in any direction; the shape shifter who is many times disguised in the Grail legends. She is both one and many, her stability pronounced in continual change.

The hero seems to be preoccupied with her as a muse of sexuality and sensuality—either in the repressed Christian texts or the other extreme: the promiscuous Welsh versions. Now, whether or not the hero is chaste and pure of heart—Galahad or Gawain—is beside the point. One either finds the knight hero a reluctant virgin who has to be reminded to hang on to his purity ("Let her chase *me*") or who is wrestling a coy but willing maiden to the floor without a commitment to her safety and security.

It seems strange that implicit and explicit sexuality is heightened in such a holy quest until we reexamine the mythic current beneath the collective unconscious—a quest to also reestablish the male's displaced female aspect, his anima yin soul. The Grail castle was at one time visible to all.

But when King Amangon raped the maiden and stole her ceremonial cup—with all his men following suit—the wells were deserted, and no one could find the entrance to the other world any longer. The kingdom lay barren and wasted, and the water dried up.

The only one who could restore the land to its original state was he who could recognize the Fisher King and the castle behind the many false reflections.

The Grail Bearer symbolizes the original maidens of the wells, who gave drink and nourishment to all. More importantly, however, she represents, like the maidens, the sovereignty of the land (the queen), which withdraws and dries up when the king forces her to his own will. He neither serves her nor gives her anything—such as commitment to status and security in the world—in return for her gifts of sensuality and sexuality.

The maimed or impotent king is unfit to rule or to be in union with the sovereignty, the potent queen. He has failed to protect the maidens and thus the queen and the mystical kingdom of love shared.

The queen appears to the hero in many guises: the hag, the virgin, the seductress, finally transforming to the queen or empress who can only dispense the sacred love nourishment to the worthy hero.

So the Quest for Grail is the quest for women. Whosoever finds her, finds the Grail.

The predominantly male yang authority rapes the land and steals sovereignty from the yin/maiden queen (symbolized by the chalice) and makes her a possession, an object. Only when the mother's son comes either to kill or heal the father can there be restoration of her original sovereignty. The Quest for the Grail can be seen as a celebration ritual of the eternal yin female who awaits the yang son to reinstate her title and restore harmony to the realm.

In some traditions, Sophia, the spirit of wisdom, is thought to be the powerful female yin part of God's soul. Just like the Grail Bearer and Mary Magdalene, Sophia is symbolized by a dove. It was Sophia who sent her own spirit to the Garden of Eden in order to tempt Adam and Eve to disobey God. As we know, they chose to eat of the Tree of Knowledge to be like God, condemning mankind to forever struggle to reclaim paradise lost.

The early Christian movement (which took Gnostic root) held Sophia in great love and devotion, building her the greatest shrine at Constantinople. She also appeared in the Jewish Kabbalah as the Shekinah of God. The patriarchs of Rome, like the mullahs of the Middle East, dismissed Sophia as a foolish woman who knew nothing.

The Gnostic gospels (which predate the canonized gospels of the church) insisted that Jesus gave the help of the kingdom of heaven to Mary Magdalene, not Peter, which is why Peter was so jealous of Mary and all other women. This orientation was not at all unique to early Christianity. Before the patriarchs of Islam arrived in the seventh century, Arabia had been matriarchal for a millennium or so. At Mecca, the goddess Sheba had been worshiped in the form of the black anionic stone, which is now enshrined at Kaaba.

The influence of Sophia was widespread throughout Europe in the Middle Ages. However, she had to be hidden from the Inquisition within alchemical treatises or astrological manuscripts (including the first tarot cards). In the Middle Ages, we find secret symbols and obscure illustrations that carried that feminine message in visual language, which baffled orthodox theologians.

A new sense of balanced religiousness was spearheaded by the Catbar's alternative Church of Love and secretly supported by the Templars, the cults of Mary Magdalene, the Black Virgin of Madonna Inspiritus, and the writers of the Grail romances.

The mission of the Grail was revolutionary and radical, to say the least.

4

THE WASTELAND

Easterners who had not fully embraced Islam and who still worshiped the Goddess maintained that the great deserts had been caused by the renunciation of the Great Mother who had withdrawn her fertility from the land. The deep fear was that the same would happen in Europe.

The symbolic wasteland, on the other hand, was far more pernicious. This was the landscape of spiritual death, in which religious concepts had become so divorced from feelings and real-life experiences. In the twelfth and thirteenth centuries, the coming of the Mahdi, or the desired knight, was identified. This depended on tradition and region, as the second coming of Christ—as the long-awaited awakening of Arthur, Merlin, or some other reinstatement of the hero.

In virtually every account of the Grail legend, the final goal of the quest is either the reestablishment or the transformation of the wasteland into paradise. But in the Grail myth, the original paradise state of both the land and the inner realm of characters have been lost. Each of the various accounts gives reasons for both its loss and what the hero had to do to restore the earthly Eden.

The healing of the wound can only be brought about by the radical transformation of the individual into a whole and complete being, including male yang and female yin natures—the dominant active and the cooperative passive energy systems.

Just as schizophrenic divisions permeate all aspects of this dominator system—and each split forms new hierarchies of dependence—the state tends to separate from the spirit, the sacred from the secular, the male from the female, individual from individual, the left-hand hemisphere from the right hand, and the individual from his or her own decision-making process.

The very nature of this system is coercive, manipulative, competitive, violent, and warlike.

To the mystic, the bulk of the system is seen as the development of a false and separate sense of self, called ego. Distrust, fear, and a death-oriented vision are common features that arise from this condition. While the clouds were only gathering at the time of the writing of the Grail legends, Europe was soon to experience darkness—the Inquisition, the heretic hunts, and the Black Death—but not before the Grail Legends had warned about the coming of the wasteland and the loss of balance.

The compulsion to return to that sacred state of the garden can be seen as one of the most powerful of human longings. Paradise myths throughout the world are strikingly similar, as if they actually tell of a time when we celebrated life, the land, laughter, love, and the light of the spirit, which appeared to permeate all things.

We come full circle in the theme of the Grail, repeated in all the Celtic accounts; it is a union of the two principles of the Goddess and the Hero-King. This is the foundational condition of paradise. The one great dream of man is to create a paradise to his own specifications that contain all the desirable elements of the social, economic, and spiritual worlds but none of the undesirable ones.

The trouble has been that the hierarchical paradigm of the last five thousand years remains so firmly in place that our inner conditioning does not allow us to step outside of its conceptual framework. So, even those with the best intentions often fall prey to the dominator syndrome.

From the time of the Spartans of ancient Greece, few attempts have lasted long. It is an indication of the strength of the female yin principle that the Shaker communities of America have lasted the longest. Founded by a woman and based on cooperation, equality, and shared living, the Shakers almost created their dream, but they sadly avoided grasping that prickly subject for all spiritual seekers—sex.

They solved it by pretending it was not there. They became celibate, which *is not* always synonymous with paradise or likely to produce legacy.

We are faced with the same question that the hero had to ask: "What ails thee, Uncle?" If a real hero had asked the people of Europe in the twelfth and thirteenth centuries, then perhaps the horrors of the Crusades, the Inquisition, and the suppression of female power and potency might have been avoided.

As it was, questions were crushed, and the scales instead crashed toward the side of male dominance. Europe at that time (as with the Middle East today) became a wasteland for eight hundred years.

The same nightmare today still surrounds us in war, fanatical religious terrorism and ethnic strife, empty materialism, a technology that divides us, and an undercurrent of violent means to solve our problems.

There is a sense of hopelessness in a future that is predicted to be overpopulated and over-polluted. All the ecological Band-Aids in the world will not help the deeply ingrained attitudes we have of dominating and controlling nature herself. It is indeed a man's world and a woman's universe. Yang without yin, material things without air, and humanity without love must find a way to blend if paradise is to be achieved on earth.

PART 1

I-ness

5

THE WOUNDS OF THE INDIVIDUAL SELF

Leo Tolstoy said, "Everyone thinks of changing the world, but no one thinks of changing himself."

Until we face our own demons and take responsibility for who and what we are, we cannot grow into our highest aspect of being. We are stalled on the shores of spiritual evolution, because we continue to seesaw back and forth in a world of pendulum-swinging dualities. Religions are still at war with science, and world leaders still settle their scores with blood.

We are no longer just apathetic; we have grown comfortably numb.

We have accepted the tactics of fear and guilt. We have accepted the hollowness of our own existence in a society of acceptable and polite untruths. We are in need of accounting. The time spent on being the victim is wasted. It is time for the hero yang to emerge in the individual spirituality of knowing that there is a better way. Only by risking all that is considered known in our fantasy of tradition can we boldly seek new ground.

We will not evolve further past the healing wound of the repression of yin energy woman until the yang energy hero is reinstated and the individual begins to find both retraction and revocation of the dominator's use of guilt and shame within our accountability.

6

WOUNDED KINGS AND HEROES

So far, the need to call attention to the loss of the feminine yin principle has somewhat overshadowed the reinstatement of the masculine yang hero principle. In Grail legend, the hero is selected by the female principle and is called upon to either heal the wounded king or to *replace* him.

In examining the archetypal hero, the most common current in the hero quest is that of leaving one condition in order to discover a richer or more mature condition. In essence, the hero's yang quest is that of transformation (i.e., higher consciousness).

"The most important thing is this: to be able at any moment to sacrifice what we are for what we could become" (Charles Dubois).

The hero is one who gives his life over to something greater than himself, which can transpire only when the hero is no longer singularly identified with the ego.

This is also the path of the mystic. Both the hero and the mystic have to die to ego, die to an *idea* of who they are (ego). Only then can they can be reborn as something else and something greater. Only when the individual identification ceases to be solely ego-driven can transformation happen.

7

LESSONS OF THE EMPTY VESSEL

The key to any heroic act is in letting go of the self to strip down to the emptiness of the vessel that can then be filled with something greater. That *something greater* is usually a cause.

Personal ambition still lies within the category of the ego. This is the death and resurrection of the lower aspect into the higher aspect.

In Grail legend, Parzival has to allow the fool to die in order for the new Parzival to take his seat at the Roundtable. The origin of the word *passion* comes from the Latin *passio* meaning *to suffer*. We are therefore willing to suffer for something we have passion for. Only through the twin pillars of doubt and love can passion be balanced with compassion, and compassion arrives only when one is truly humble. To be humble is not some pious cloak. It is genuine, it is real, and it bears no laminate cover.

But today, men and women are impotent. We seem to be living in a world where power and potency are measured in dollars. It is a world of violence, a world where lies are not only acceptable, but also expected.

The focus is on economic and political agendas, initiated by those at the top, at the pinnacle, religiously in the Middle East and politically in the West. The illusion of the hero, the false hero, is dominated by time, money, and information. We have lost our sense of the mystical, the spiritual, and the internal.

Yang left-brain corporate linear thinking has taught us to revere bottom lines and end results instead of the almighty creative feminine yin force that is the wellspring to all things that progress in the universe. Our faith has been crushed; our trust is broken. Inspiration has gone dry only because we continue to think in step-by-step strategies or methods that are supposed to bring about guaranteed and immediate results.

We failed to hold the great synthesis of yin and yang, world and universe, useful and lovable, man and woman that are the source of the wellspring. We want a manual of instructions, not a process. But wisdom and creation are never found this way.

We sense that we are in a hopeless state, and we will remain thus until the hero is once again evoked.

8

THE ULTIMATE PATH OF THE HEROINE: TO HEAL THE WOUND

The cruelest of legacies has been cast upon our heads: religions that teach that we, especially women, are born sinners.

In Fundamentalist Orthodox Christian and Muslim dogma, there appears to be no way we can redeem our stigma or essentially change our sinful nature.

In this, the wounded king is revealed; in trying to change ourselves into what we were not, what was essentially within the essence of the beauty of our own creation, we have become a people guilty and schizophrenic-like. The cure then, is to evolve into our highest aspect, trust in our own inner nature, and then act upon it. When the hero has honestly faced the demons and produced out of himself a higher aspect, he is ready to seek the Grail, acting upon his or her natural flow.

Then, and only then, the universe reaches down and fills the empty space that was left by the first aspect, the false or incomplete aspect. By resurrecting, and through cause that raises the consciousness, the hero strips away the gravity of the misused ego and can rise to the higher frequencies of wisdom and magnetic attraction. He becomes the leader, the yang energy, the true charismatic.

This is not because of his dollars or rank but because he now resonates within the scheme of the universe—the yin energy itself—volunteering himself as an instrument of a bigger picture. This differs from the castrated martyr. The martyr sacrifices self, but in doing so, has drawn the universe back into its crimson pendulum swing of yin and yang. It might produce results for a time, but the great pendulum will swing back and reclaim its imbalance.

The hero understands that he must forsake—*for* sake (purpose, cause) but also for his own sake. This is the difference, and it raises him from a lower level of love and passion to that of a higher level, which is the frequency just before transformation.

9

TRANSFORMATION

The separation from our own yang nature has cut men from the female yin principle that exists within them, that which we call the anima soul of man. It has prevented access to their inner receptive spirit. The twentieth century was a manifestation of the wasteland. Each of us carries the microcosm of that wasteland within us, because we have been conditioned and programmed to do so.

The Grail legend reveals a path that must be taken by the individual—a path that is internal and a way back to the universe of the spiritual. In giving over our lives to something larger than ourselves, we evoke within ourselves that which can *save us*. It is simply allowing the greater part of what has been severed within us to fill the emptiness left when the false self (misused ego) is left behind.

Parzival remained true to what he loved, true to his quest in finding something bigger than himself; he was humble and therefore worthy to receive it. He did this by stopping his thinking in terms of others' ideas. He stopped drawing the lines at black and white and accepted the whole.

The early English hero, Beowulf, claims his strength was in knowing that there was darkness within him and he embraced its wisdom and did not act on its impunity. Therefore, he was able to conquer Grendel and Grendel's mother, even without his sword. The spirit of the valley is the spirit of emptiness; "an empty hollow between two peaks" (Lao Tzu). It is the ravine between two mountain peaks, which must be filled just as *perce a val* is symbolic of the piercing of that valley.

The Grail is a vessel of emptiness, because it is the principle of receptivity, the yin within yang, and so it can be all things to all men. It was the Grail that was said to have nourished everyone with what they desired.

Every time Parzival lets go of the reins of his horse and relaxes in the saddle, accepting that wherever he goes is fine, (intuitively), it turns out for the best. But the moment he tried to take control and impose his *superior* belief (misused ego) upon the natural order, he becomes lost in the wasteland. Parzival had to let go all that had been "programmed" into him in order to let this enter him. It was only when he ceased to be the greatest knight—on the most sacred quest, seeking the most important object in the world, and rejected the greatest God religions could offer—that it found him.

The ego is the mainstay of a dominator system. The Grail legend describes the action of the ego and its desperate need to be extraordinary. If we only see the wasteland around us, we are blind to its perpetrator: ego, which denies us introspection and gives birth to its own creative infertility. We cease to grow.

Those men and women who seek the golden cup and choose to be identified with its glory or seize its power for their own sake have failed to understand the power of the Grail at all. For it is the emptiness within, yearning to be filled with the sacred, that is the healing. As in the beginning, darkness had its longing; the emptiness is also an expressed desire to be filled with something greater. But to want or desire without moving forward, without conscious objective of positive growth, is to die in spirit.

Thus, one must be in quest of or seek beyond what one already knows as an individual, beyond what is orthodox or traditionally accepted as a society, in order to progress to a new state. "And in the master's chambers, we gather for the feast. They stab it with their steely knives, but they just can't kill the beast. We are all just prisoners here of our own device." ("Hotel California" by the Eagles).

As long as we cannot accept ourselves as we are—or we accept ourselves in the wallow of our own egocentric and blind deficiency, *or* we continue to blame external forces for our own failures—we are doomed to live in the wasteland of our lost dreams and desires, wants and not wants. What we cannot accept as being natural and positive, we fail to redeem on our own, rising past the circumstances of defiled sinner into a realm beyond.

We must ask ourselves "What ails thee, Uncle?" and remedy what is deficient within us on our own, without being programmed into someone else's belief system—just as Parzival had to literally fight against the weapons created from his own errors.

Then miraculously, in a single moment, the Grail is empty—and in the next, it is filled with wonder. The glory of all and everything is within our vision and the potential of our grasp.

It is the unlocking, the decoding of the inner helix, that is unfurled, and we find ourselves very much capable of awakening to frequencies that take us to the external gardens and amber glow of paradise on earth. We awaken to invisible spectrums of unnamed aurora borealis light in the universe and to the primal harmonies of patterns hidden in chaos for those yang men and yin women courageous enough to be themselves, to live the hero's life in *I-ness*.

10

Do I Need You or Want You?

In today's world, self-esteem is a hard thing to achieve. We have world issues, city problems, ethnic chaos, and religious confusion impacting families. Addictions of every kind are rampant, including television, computer, porn, gambling, eating, drinking, drugs, and sex, along with dysfunctions created by mental illness.

Nietzsche said, "If it doesn't kill you, it will strengthen you." A lot of kids are killed today—physically, mentally, and, worst of all, emotionally. Those who are strengthened by problem solving are few and far between. Being a healthy man or woman today is a lonely miracle. Loneliness often causes a man or woman to bend into a pretzel to *fit* with an unhealthy man or woman.

How many times have I heard in my offices "I don't want to be alone" or "Being with him (or her) is better than being alone." The only problem with these rationalizations is that when a healthy man or woman sells out to be with an unhealthy man or woman, both become unhealthy. In my forty plus years as a therapist, I have never been able to help a good, virtuous, spiritual (able to love self and others) man lead an unhealthy woman to a higher spiritual (lovable) level.

There are *no* male muses! *Why*, you ask? It is helpful to refer to Carl Jung's theory of anima and animus, also demonstrated in the ancient Chinese concept of yin-yang energy balance. Within every female, there is her animus element of intuition, self-assertion, and masculinity. And within every male there is his anima—his sensitive, instinctive, responsive feminine aspect.

Girls feel-think, with feeling comprising their feminine experience of sensitivity, warmth, and responsiveness. If a father does not play the role of Daddy by cherishing her exterior feminine (or yin) side, then he will instead become a *father* by generally promoting her interior masculine (or yang) aspect.

This results in a woman who cannot cherish her own feelings, a woman who is more into performance than she is into process—in short, an unfeminine woman. And she will have difficulty responding from her female side to any man later in life.

Example

This is our first example and with that an explanation is in order. The term *rape* is ordinarily used in reference to the physical, sexual violation of another human being, but there are other kinds of rape that violate the mind and spirit of a human being in ways that may or may not leave physical marks. Jails and mental hospitals are full of people who bear no physical marks to show the rape that has taken place. I have termed this more subtle form of rape *conversational rape*.

> Dialogue
> Supermom: Oh, come on. One more drink (or helping) won't hurt you.
> Victim: Well, I guess one more drink (or helping) won't hurt me. Ha, ha!
> *Rape!*

Rape Analysis

For a man, woman, or child with poor self-esteem, food, drink, or drugs are a way to give that person *thing*-strokes to replace the people-strokes they fear. We all need stroke stimulation, either positive or negative, and we also need to structure our time to obtain strokes.

Strokes come in three varieties. The highest quality strokes are those that can bring the greatest pleasure or pain, and they come from people—especially those with whom we are intimate. The second level of strokes comes from nature: animals, plants, the sky, sand, grass, and the outdoors in general. Many people use outdoor nature strokes to maintain a major portion of their stroke ecology. They structure their time to include walking, jogging, running, swimming, gardening, or some other form of outdoor exercise.

The lowest quality stroke comes from *things*. These replace human interaction, and include any impulsive compulsive activity like food, drink, drugs, money, or sex for sex's sake. Children who learn too early that their world is filled with pain due to poor family relationships often turn to things to fill their world in a safer way. This bad habit grows with them into adulthood, leaving them unskilled in communicating wants and not-wants. They exist only as victims. They have been conversationally raped.

Pain-filled homes produce two kinds of children. There are those who believe that pain is the normal state of existence and that pleasure should be avoided. Others believe pain will kill them and that they therefore must be sedated with alcohol, sugar, or drugs. I call them the pain addict and the no-pain addict. They very often marry each other later in life in order to maintain emotional balance.

The pain addict victim will discount compliments. This person will stay in jobs, marriages, and relationships of negative quality. They generally see only the dark side on all occasions. They are not pleasant people to be around.

The no-pain addict may seem cheerful when all is going well or while they are sedated with chemicals. At the first sign of anxiety or pain, however, they panic and run for emotional cover. Thus, they never learn how to protect themselves from conversation rape.

Straight Talk

Both the pain and the no-pain addict need to be reeducated in how to get the higher quality stroke from humans. They need to be taught how to communicate their wants and not-wants verbally, in a rational, free manner. Very often they must be taught that pain is a symptom, not a disease. It is an indication that change is needed or that change is in progress. Pain will never destroy them or anyone else.

In order to become fully functioning adults, these persons must learn the lesson that unless we each are willing to give and take pain, we may never learn how to take care of ourselves or relate to one another. We each can hurt ourselves through mismanagement of pain, but it is our responsibility, not theirs, if we do so.

By learning to talk straight—and to express our wants and not-wants without resorting to trickery, intimidation, and guilt or subtle gamesmanship—we learn to channel our normal negative feelings into positive energy. Anger, guilt, sadness, resentment, or frustration, for example, that flow through our sober thinking can motivate us to act rationally and productively.

No healthy person wishes to sustain a negative feeling. As we grow into fully actualized human beings, we realize a profound truth: the healthy way to overcome a negative feeling is to make a positive decision, followed by action or inaction as soon as possible. You do this by asking yourself, *What do I have that I don't want?* and *What do I want that I don't have?*

There are two main motivational mechanisms in our lives: pain, which drives us away from those things we do not want, and pleasure, which draws us toward those things that we do want. A good combination of human, nature, and thing-strokes lends itself to a balanced life based not on pain, but on pleasure.

11

DO I WANT TO BE THE BREADWINNER (LAID) OR THE HOMEMAKER (PAID)?

Before the women's liberation movement began in the '60s, men were expected to be the breadwinners who managed the world—so it was indeed a man's world. They needed to repress their feminine (loving yin soul or anima) to pay bills, fight wars, and protect women and children. They paid dearly, and some still pay for this repression with heart disease, strokes, and chronic illness.

Women, on the other hand, were expected to become homemakers, and for those who worked, their careers were relationship-centered; they were nurses, teachers, maids, and secretaries. Women were in charge of the abstract, the air of love we all breathe, the universe of human interaction. The repressed masculine side, the yang soul of every woman, screamed for equality in the world of money, power, and prestige. They paid dearly when the women's lib war began. Where did they pay? They paid in the loving areas of marriage and children. I like to say, "The women's movement brought us independence, but it did not bring us love."

Instead of joining forces with men, women during the women's movement competed with men in their world of money, power, and prestige.

The men's liberation movement began in the United States on September 11, 2001. At that terrible moment in our history, we all became viscerally aware that we needed men and their bodies to face the reality of earth, fire, death, and dirt. Men, women, and children lived who otherwise would have died if policemen and firemen hadn't led them out of harm's way. Other men, women, and children died because intellectual communication systems failed.

Survival for many meant running away from danger. Others died because they waited for instructions. A new style of hero emerged—a man who may not be a financially successful giant but who cared about helping humans live. Women again looked at the physically good man who worked with his body and not just his money-making brain. Safety became more valuable than financial security.

It is a man's world of money, power, and prestige—even when the "men" are in women's bodies. It is a woman's universe of love, relatedness, physical pleasure, and feeling safe, even when the "women" are in men's bodies. September 11 was a demonstration of the yin, anima, lovable feminine men's gift to the world. He is worthy of respect and cherishing, even if he doesn't have the education, money, or stature in society that others have.

There is a place for all types of men and women. Some will choose careers over relationships; others, the reverse. Homemakers and breadwinners complement each other; they need not compete. Women's lib pushed women, some reluctantly, into breadwinning; September 11, 2001 pulled *real men* into homemaking and protecting. It's time for men to defend their choices and set standards, just as women have.

Conversational Rape Example: Office Politics

Conversation:
Supervisor: No excuses—just get it done today!
Clerk: But I can't get it all done today because—
Supervisor: Well, if you can't do your job, we'll get someone else around here who can.

Rape!

Rape Analysis

People in authority have power, but sometimes the way they exercise their power indicates a lack of personal potency within themselves. Careers and jobs that stress one-up boss and one-down employee often attract needy, question-mark people. Legal careers, careers in law enforcement, the military, medicine, politics—these are the most obvious places where this happens. But subtler, more power-sensitive careers in teaching, the ministry, and the junior/senior executive ladder in business also promote one-upmanship. Needy people, out of fear of not trusting themselves, focus more on survival rather than on success. They often promote and invite domination, using conversational rape of mendicancy. Their talk is always "May I, please?" or "Would it be all right?" instead of "I want— may I?"

On the other hand, there are bosses who cover their insecurity with shows of domination: "You should do it my way, or else!" With these tactics, they are indicating that they do not believe in their ability to successfully negotiate their wants. They decide instead to use a power play. Ironically, such a power-centered person often goes home to become a powerless pawn in his or her marriage, a Daisy or David Daffodil.

This is especially prevalent in the "god" professions. Doctors, lawyers, ministers, therapists, and teachers can easily take advantage of the ignorance and fear in their patients, clients, and students. When their actions promote insecurity, they perpetuate the rape system in society in a significant way, as these high-profile careers symbolically duplicate the parental roles that launched the individual's identity system in the first place.

Straight Talk

On the positive side of this coin, these parental careers have the great potential to do much to promote I-centeredness and emotional stability in the persons they deal with throughout their careers, because these professions represent current parental messages, properly tailored to replace prior negative communication in the lives of their patients, clients, and employees.

Such a positive office request might be as follows:

Rational Conversation:

Supervisor: I want this job done today. Will you do it?
Clerk: I want to do it today, and I will, unless something interferes. I'll let you know by two o'clock this afternoon if I'm not able to get it done.
Supervisor: Fine, if you need some help, ask.

In this dialogue, the same request was made, but in a more potent and healthier way for both parties.

12

CAN TWO MAKE AND KEEP COMMITMENTS?

The result of not keeping commitments was, and is, the neglect of home, family, children, and the art of loving abstractly. Today our world is under attack on a material, concrete level—September 11, terrorism, and loss of freedoms. It will be up to the men to set the standards for women and children. As long as men allow women and children to compete with them for leadership through seduction, especially sexual, we are lost.

There are no non-committable men. Some men want a safe, virtuous, sensual, and sexual harbor after a day in the world. Some men can set up their own bachelor pad, cook, clean, and decorate—or let their places be messy. Others want that harbor to be created by a loved one—mom, daughter, wife, or another guy. A cave is a safe place to rest, be nourished, and play. Because our brains are built to think and feel in unison, we women can often build our own caves, while right-handed men often must bring in a loving right-lobe, yin feminine energy man or woman to build a cave for them to come home to.

Only women can be non-committable in the area of loving self and others virtuously. The way a woman gets what she wants is by saying no to immoral, unethical, and illegal behavior on the part of her man or her children.

When a man asks for concrete gifts of sex and money from a woman, and she gives it to him without regard for her own integrity—her own virtue, her own spirituality—she is competing in the world of men, *not* being a woman in charge of loving. Nurturing through giving, protecting, and cherishing is a masculine skill, not a feminine one. Receiving, being available to receive, and *respecting* the giver who protects and cherishes is a feminine skill, not a masculine one.

13

AM I A SPIRITUAL OR ONLY A RELIGIOUS MAN OR WOMAN?

As women became "men" in the corporate world, men became "feminine" in the personal world of romance. "Here's my card, honey. Call me" became the male version of the old hankie- drop of Grandma's time, and women with newfound power were calling but not liking the results.

Hank, a 42-year-old former semipro baseball player, handed his advertising business card to Emilie, a thirty-five-year-old advertising executive for a women's magazine. They met at lunch time in a cafeteria line. Eyes met, bodies tingled, and the chase was on. "Call me at home," he said, as he wrote his number on the back of the card.

She called the next evening. She would have called the same day, but she had a duty date with another new man, Tom, whom she had met through a friend. The date with Tom was *boring*. Her mind was on Hank. She thought about calling him at his office but rethought that idea. *He obviously wants me in his personal life, not business. I'll wait 'til the evening to call*, she thought.

"Hi, this is Emilie," she said when he answered the phone.

"Hi, Emilie. How are you?" he replied.

Emilie's heart was pounding.

"Look, Emilie," he said. "I'm a little busy right now."

She could hear a woman's voice in the background: "Come on, Hank, we're going to be late."

"Could you call me at my office tomorrow?" he asked.

Emilie was crestfallen. She knew intellectually that he was a single man on a date, but her feelings were hurt. Why had he put his home number on the card and now asked her to call the office? At her next therapy appointment, she asked me what I could make of it. I told her that he had given her a mixed message: "Call me" and then, "Go away." He was safe and secure in her wanting to call him. His feelings had been protected against rejection. She had taken the risk of rejection.

In the future, when a man gives you his business card, call him for business reasons, even on a false pretext. Don't call him at home. Give him your card, or write your number on the back of his card and give it back to him.

Today's man is as sensitive to rejection as any woman. Today's liberated woman has been taught to reach out, be courageous, and go for it, and men are more than willing to support your risk taking. You must decide in each situation whether you want to chase or be chased, give or receive and give back, lead or follow, act or be passive.

Women are still confused by men who lead them into being masculine against their true feelings of wanting to be cherished as receivers, not respected as giving women. Equality was the goal, narcissism the problem.

Helen was furious with her husband, Jim. Last week he took her to the softball game he played in weekly, and she loved the other wives and girlfriends and the party afterward. This week she asked him if he were going to take her again. "No, the guys want to do a man's only beer party at Hal's bachelor pad after the last game of the season."

"Why do you men always get your way? Why can't you think of our feelings more?" she asked, pouting in that way she does her pouting— acting formal and cold, polite like a servant. Jim's feelings of excitement about the party were dampened, and Helen felt righteous rage. Jim knew she talked about it to her mom and sister, and he felt sad and angry and drank too much, getting himself into more hot water.

Helen believed, as did her mom and two sisters, that their husbands should respect women's wants and needs. It was his job to help her be happy, so she could and would respect him as a good husband. Helen was a narcissist, a permanently single woman who needed a man to be her daddy, a *zero* who tended to her life's needs, wants, thoughts, and feelings at the expense of her husband's own life, thoughts, and feelings.

She was the new-age matriarchal version of the old game of patriarchal male domination.

Women's liberation has freed some women to be matriarchal men, and some men are allowing themselves to be castrated into helplessly dominated women.

Everyone who wants respect for their thinking, speaking, and action *and* cherishing for their feelings, physical needs for sex, and affection is a narcissist. As long as you are single and not a parent, you are a healthy, independent, individualized, and actualized person. The problems arise when you want both respect *and* cherishing from your significant other, wife, husband, or child. Two narcissists can disco but not waltz.

To waltz, you must lead or follow in each dance. Negotiated equity and the exchange of gifts (sex and dollars) allow intimacy and stop game playing, fear-based intimidation, and guilt-based seduction. Every healthy boy, girl, man, or woman is ambisexual, i.e., both masculine (money, power, prestige) and feminine (feelings, physical, loving).

Example: Man to Man

Conversation:
Bill: Up for a hot game of racquetball after work?
Joe: No, I really haven't played in so long. I'd bust something.
Bill: Hah, you're just afraid you'll get creamed!
Rape!

Rape Analysis

Bill and Joe are prime examples of what I call Macho Super-Jock and David Daffodil.

Macho Super-Jock Bill is the man who's been raised in a man-centered home, where total emphasis was on his masculine performance capabilities. His feminine process system has been suppressed, described variously as *faggy* and *inappropriate*, and he's been indoctrinated with the idea: "Boys don't do that. That's for girls." David Daffodil Joe has obviously grown accustomed to using his feelings over his brains, because his brains have been discounted, and he cannot trust them for an up-to-snuff performance.

One man has been castrated on the top of the think mountain, and the other has been castrated at the bottom of the feel valley. Men raised to express themselves exclusively as males, with pressure put on them for performance, respond in one of two ways. Either they overdo and consequently overact, like Macho Bill did, or they underdo their masculinity and lose faith in themselves, as with Daffodil Joe. Because neither of these men has their anima feelings under control, they cannot be considered true males. They are both half-men. Their anima feelings have not been incorporated within their thinking, performance, masculine center.

In our culture, we admire those who produce more, but what price do we pay for teaching our men to do nothing but perform? What prize do we garner?

The price we pay is that these men become insensitive, they die earlier, and they don't enjoy their lives as much as they could.

There are three levels of stroke systems: *people*, who are highest quality, *nature* second, and *things* third. Naturally, if men are taught that people are not sources of strokes and that they don't have access to nature, they are not going to till the soil; men are then going to go into their offices for the sole purpose of producing that green stuff called money. Men are going to be encouraged to go out and buy those cars and houses as the only way to express love to the people they care about.

Bill is a man who watches football and other sports as a vicarious *feel* vehicle. Athletics put Bill in touch with other performance males. Athletics afford men such as Bill an opportunity to touch men and to feel and perform in a competitive arena.

But for the man who does not allow himself enough time to experience his body, actively watching others is a poor second-best alternative.

For Daffodil Joe, his over-civilized castrated-feeling approach to life may allow him easier access to the feeling world of women. Thus, to earn a living he joins women in feeling-centered occupations, such as cosmetology, interior design, fashion, or the arts. Even teaching and nursing could be included here.

But the price he pays in overbalance is harsh.

The goal of every human being is balance and integration, meaning appropriate behavior based on feeling secure internally, thinking logically, and acting appropriately.

Bill and Joe are fundamentally out of balance and need assistance in realigning themselves.

If you tracked Macho Bill long enough, you would find that he would eventually run into the hard wall of reality. Without proper internal balance, Bill will ultimately have his wife run out on him, or he'll lose his job, or he'll get physically sick. Any of these factors will undermine his performance abilities, and he will then go into a depression arising from repressed feelings.

Daffodil Joe is a man straining to perform appropriately, who is just not equal to the task. Very often, he acts cowardly or withdraws from reality. He becomes an alcoholic in order to escape his intuitive inadequacy, or he becomes a violent man seeking release through intimidating others. He blows up, or he blows inward. He is likely to be a latent or an actual homosexual, his true sexuality retreating out of fear of women and their hurtful power.

Straight Talk

Macho Super-Jock was raped as a young person—raped of his permission to experience his feelings. It's not necessary to always perform. He can process a feeling as Joe and learn to enjoy the feelings of play as well as the pride in performance. David Daffodil was raped as a young person in that he was not given enough respect for his problem-solving performance ability. As a result, his feelings constantly swamp his thinking, and consequently he forfeits both his self-esteem and self-worth. He's not only poorly motivated; he's also a poor performer. A more rational back-and-forth about racquetball might go something like this:

Bill: How about a game of racquetball, Joe?

Joe: Okay, but let me warn you, my game's not really up to par these days.

Bill: Oh, that's okay. I'm just glad for the game.

Joe: Thanks, and I'll do my best and give you a run for your money.

Now, the two men are more human, seeking the goals of balance, integration, and appropriate behavior based on feeling secure internally, thinking logically, and acting appropriately.

Example: Woman to Woman

Conversation:

Alice: You really should get your hair colored, Mary. It would make you look years younger.

Mary: Do you really think so, Alice? I don't know anything about such things.

Alice: I'll make an appointment with my hairdresser, dear. We're going to get you all fixed up.

Rape!

Rape Analysis

Once again both people have been raped, either currently or in the past. But in this particular case, the rape is subtler.

Being women, both of these ladies are given to feeling statements. Alice portrays in her exhibition of language what I call Super-Mom Bertha Balls. Simply stated, she's doing the active giving for and to another person in order to exercise control. She is a lady who was taught, probably by a father who was performance-oriented and by a mother who did perform as supermom or critical mom, or didn't perform at all, choosing the role of Daisy Daffodil. One of these extremes encouraged Alice into performing. As a result, she's determined to rescue poor little Mary, who doesn't know how to fix her hair. She is, in effect, overextending herself.

Mary, on the other hand, is playing stupid Daisy Daffodil. By being stupid, Mary can seduce Alice into rescuing her. Alice invited action on the part of Mary, and this perpetuates Mary's self-recognized powerful passivity. I make a statement here—that may sound incongruous but is nonetheless true—that the passive person is the one in control in this situation, the powerful one, and that the person who is in the active role is generally the more helpless. Alice is being raped at this time because she is in effect being seduced into doing a performance to take care of Mary. Mary has been raped in the past, and is now in the process of raping Alice. Mary does this by being the helpless, inactive, but passively powerful woman

Straight Talk

Women are predominantly process-oriented, feeling-centered, body-centered human beings who use their brains to take care of their feelings, their bodies, and their processes. So let's examine the dialogue between two healthy, individuated women.

The dialogue for this situation would first have Alice requesting Mary's permission to make a suggestion about her appearance. When Mary gives her a go-ahead, Alice's comment to Mary might be, "I suggest that you think about having your hair colored. Are you willing to do that?" Mary would then respond, "I appreciate your caring about my hair. I want to think about that before I take action. I appreciate your caring about my looks."

Let's spend some time examining the roles of women in today's society. It is my opinion that we are at the apex of an emergence of a new entity for women and their process/performance integration.

In the past, our concern has been directed toward women's performance in the home, and we traditionally discounted women's capabilities in performing in the man's world of, for example, banking, sales, construction, or top executive strategizing. We gave women permission to perform in feminine occupations like nursing and teaching, but not to operate in spheres like engineering and other traditional male bastions.

Today, thanks to the women's lib movement—which is basically an economic shift more than a psychological movement—we have seen women move into many if not most occupations formerly dominated by men. Women have gained more legal, business, professional, and economic privileges and "have made tremendous strides in increasing their labor market experience and their skills" ("Gender Pay Gap: Recent Trends and Explanations," Council of Economic Advisors Issue Brief, April 2015). This is a good thing, for both women and men. There is a firm sense of equality in the workplace.

There have come to light, however, unintended consequences of this paradigm shift in our society. One of these consequences is a psychological problem, that of extremism. There are career women who are performance-oriented. These Bertha Balls and Supermoms have begun to face-off with more traditional housewives who are process-oriented Daisy Daffodils, and each camp has become highly critical of the other.

To be sure, some women are becoming too performance-oriented. They are losing the female priority system and not concentrating on process. The typical women's libber, with all the inappropriate aggressive manifestations, is really a woman hater. She has voluntarily entered into competition with men for work in a man's world, competing with both men and other women in a male world for a male position and the prize of economic independence. But the psychological costs of this competition have become greater liabilities than the financial gain and the achievement of economic equality.

On the other hand, Daisy Daffodil may be choosing to overreact by absenting herself from all competition by staying home. Daisy has elected not to test her abilities in the marketplace, responding to a feeling of repulsion at the harshness of the woman's libber. Sadly, Daisy pays her own price in staying underdeveloped as a woman.

The appropriately blended woman is one who predominantly knows what she wants based on her own unique sensitivity and then goes after it. She does not allow herself to be stampeded into competitive performance based on somebody else's direction. She does not allow herself to be intimidated into leaving her home if she does not want to leave it. The appropriately blended woman can be as good a woman at home as she can be in an office.

Too many times, home-oriented women are discounted and intimidated into leaving their homes based on their women's lib sister accusing them of not being progressive women. But staying home and performing at home may be exactly what the home-oriented woman wants. Some women who are out there and pushing for performance are going at it in such an insensitive, controversial, and antagonistic way that they're creating bad feelings, not only in business and society but also among home-oriented okay women.

Women in today's world would do well to continue to process their own feelings, whatever they may be. Good use of their brain would be in channeling those feelings. My want is to give women permission to perform rationally, logically, and to see themselves as good women, anywhere they work, inside or outside the home.

In times now long past, women were seen as the other half of their men. Men went out to work and earn money to provide for the nest. Women stayed at home and created a stable environment in which to raise a brood. They were called *homemakers* (not *housewives*), a description of their chosen occupation. With the migration of women into business and industry during the Second World War, a conflict has arisen in the old half-and-half system. Women became aware of the fact that they, too, could do well out *there*, and with this awareness came a new choice.

As women have gathered more economic power through Equal Rights Amendment (ERA)-type legislation and National Organization of Women (NOW), they have begun campaigning to "free the slaves" still at home. Just as our country exhibited confusion over Abraham Lincoln's freeing the slaves after the Civil War—and more recently the consequential racial problems of the sixties—we experienced women's issues in the seventies and eighties.

Today it has become even more complicated, as we have an entire generation of women who were raised by mothers who came into their own during those turbulent times. These young ladies have only one role model on whom they can base their sexuality: the *libber.* They have no freedom to accept or reject the more traditional woman's role, because they have no direct experience of witnessing it in their lives. Unless they are into reading historical novels or studying psychological examinations of past generations, they have only a single concept of total equality with men—process-oriented lives and the unavoidable and destructive stress that comes from competing in a man's game, both in the boardroom and in the bedroom, with tools that were never designed for such competition—namely, their feelings.

As I have pointed out before, women tend to be feeling-centered performers as opposed to men, who are thinking-centered processors. Women today are face-to-face with a major problem, and the only solution, as I see it is getting a clear idea of what the term *performance* means, for both men and women.

Being a business or industry performer is neither more nor less valuable than being a homemaker who runs a first-rate home. The basic cognitive and physical skills are still used in both areas. The only real difference is in the amount and way money is exchanged for the performance.

The businesswoman earns a salary from the company she works for. The homemaker earns her salary from the man she works for.

This may appear to be degradation and dependence to many independent-minded women. It has been recognized in the top business circles, however, that "A man at the top must have a woman at the top at home to be any good." A good man needs to have a well-run home as part of his support structure. He needs the security of a stable home environment in order to recharge his batteries from the stress of competing in the workplace. As I have said earlier, man has within himself all the anima sensitivity, vulnerability, and creativity that women have. This anima must have a place to emerge from the protective shell of masculine competency it hides in during the workday, and a safe, attractive, well-run home is the ideal environment. It can make him a truly fit and blended man.

The top-drawer homemaker is the "man" at home behind the man in business. By her homemaking efforts, she deserves half the credit and half the money for his success. In effect, she has earned her pay for the day when she has created an environment where her man can relax and be his authentic self for a time.

It is pure hyperbole on the part of the women's lib movement when they protest that women are still being dominated, used, and abused by men. A woman who elects to stay at home is not being dominated. She is being preceded by a man who sees and acknowledges all her efforts behind his leadership, as both a protector and a supporter. As he leads her into a successful lifestyle, he protects and provides—and as she follows him, she supports and comforts him. Together, they become a successful team.

When women see themselves in competition at home with their men, confusion reigns; the man is not allowed to lead, assert, protect, or provide, and his partner does not respond, follow, or offer support. The scenario is one of all chiefs and no Indians. The lamentable result of this competition for *chief* equality is that no one wins.

On the other hand, some women who do emerge as liberated in the business arena do so with the anticipation that being equal to a man is good and that happiness will somehow result from equality. The dismal dawning is that this equality brings as much stress and heartache as happiness. It also fosters blandness and leads to unclear gender roles, particularly in the social arena.

As a result, in areas both business and personal, men and women are becoming more and more confused about proper and fulfilling ways to relate to each other. Role reversals and conflicting sex role identities have become a way of life in the twenty-first century.

My premise is that all is equal and fair in performance-centered business. My own highly successful career as a woman therapist in what was originally a man's professional domain has borne this out, and it has enabled me to use my gifts, talents, and abilities to help thousands of individuals and couples find true individuation and fulfilling emotional and sexual relationships.

In those process-centered personal and sexual areas, however, women and men are differentiated in a number of physiological and psychological areas, and those core differences demand awareness and respect if we are to have successful interpersonal relationships.

The blended man tends to feel and process his way through life better when he is encouraged and supported in his assertion, leadership, teaching, protecting, providing, and active giving roles. The blended woman, similarly, tends to feel and perform better when she is encouraged and allowed to respond to her man's sensitive leadership in a protected environment. In the ideal male-female relationship, her man seeks out and cherishes her feelings in a loving, giving way. Actively, she responds to him out of respect for his skills in thinking and doing. Since she is in the power-position, it is tantamount on the part of the woman to initiate the flow of energy, by first respecting the man she has chosen to pledge her life to.

In sum, an authentic, smart woman respects her man's brains, while an authentic, smart man then cherishes his woman's feelings. Together, they negotiate to design a life that may include the woman either staying at home or going to work. Whatever the decision, they remember to honor their unique individual priorities as a man and a woman in their personal relationship.

So, women have a new cultural problem—accepting and managing the diversity of priorities between career and home orientation. These new choices also affect their relationships with their men. Resolving both of these challenges with a mutually satisfying solution seems to be a central issue of today's world.

14

WHAT IS MY TIMETABLE FOR MATING OR MARRIAGE AND FAMILY?

We can all live alone and pay our way; rarely do people have to marry or mate today. Dating rather than courting people can get your social, sensual, and sexual needs met but not build something of long-term value. Courting couples are building a life. Dating couples are playing at life. Are you courting or are you dating? That is the question.

When a man is courting, he puts his feminine gratification needs for sex second to his loving masculine needs for a relationship or family. When a man is dating he puts his human needs for sex ahead of his spiritual need for building a loving relationship or family. If he has any self-esteem, is honest with himself, and has integrity, he will tell the woman he is with—*before* sex, which he is striving for—that he wants to play with her body.

If he has low self-esteem as a giving man and he is not a virtuous man of integrity, he will intimidate her and lead her to believe he is interested in courting, when in fact he is only dating to get sexual gratification.

When a woman is courting, she puts her masculine needs for money, power, and prestige second to her feminine needs for building a loving relationship long-term, continuously and monogamously. When a woman is only dating, she puts her human needs for financial security and social status ahead of her spiritual need for building a loving relationship or family. If she has self-esteem and is honest with herself and has integrity, she will say no to non-committable, non-negotiated sexual intercourse.

If she has low self-esteem as a loving woman and is not a virtuous woman of integrity, she will seduce him with sex and lead him to believe that having fun and sex are her dating goals, when in fact she is really courting him seductively to get the money, the power, and the prestige of marriage.

I am not a moralist. I am a therapist. My job is to help people get what they need and want out of life. My job is not to tell women to be feminine homemakers or to tell men to be masculine breadwinners. I leave that to churches, ethnic groups, and righteous therapists. There are smart women who want to be the breadwinners in their relationships and wonderful loving men who want to be homemakers.

The secret is: which am I, and how do I negotiate this with him or her with integrity and love?

15

COMPLEMENTS ATTRACT, SIMILARS REPEL

Two breadwinners can make a lot of money, but who cares for the children's needs for love? The greatest victims of women's liberation are the children who lost either a homemaking mom *or* a homemaking dad. Without love, self-esteem fails.

Children under five especially need to be loved and accepted as messy, clumsy, mistake-prone, accident-prone, demanding, irritating, and often selfish. In Dr. Taibi Kahler's Miniscript, he found there are things called *drivers*, which, when practiced, will drive you crazy. These drivers are: (1) be perfect; (2) try harder; (3) hurry up; (4) please others first; and (5) be strong. Telling a child not to cry will destroy his or her self-esteem. Without any self-esteem, this broken child will grow into a broken adult who cannot love well.

The way to not go crazy is through *allowers*. Allowers are the following:

1. Instead of being perfect, be excellent. Do your best in each situation.
2. Instead of trying harder, know how much is enough—enough money, enough sex, enough property, enough power, enough TV, enough food or drink, enough exercise, and enough wasted time. People who are addicts or obsessive and compulsive don't know how much is enough, and they must artificially discipline themselves or medically control their addictions and/or compulsions.
3. Instead of *hurrying up*, work easy. Use an hour-by-hour Day-Timer to let time flow rather than a *should-do* list that pressures or distresses you. Eustress is good *want-to-do* stress. It inspires and excites but

doesn't kill you. Distress is bad *should-do* stress. It produces cortisol, which ruins your major organ systems and kills you early. Darwin's message about the survival of the fittest rings true.

4. Pleasing others first is good for charity but not for favors. No favor goes unpunished. Charity is what you do for people who cannot do for themselves (babies, the old, and the sick). Favors are what you do for people who *can* do for themselves, but you don't want them to be independent, so you interfere and do it for them—helping them be dependent on you.

5. Instead of being strong, be open to learning new ways of living and loving. Read books, do classes, go to church or temple, and go to therapy or school. Get a mentor or a coach. You need self-esteem to be a potent individual.

> Without self-esteem, integrity and virtue fail.
> Without integrity and virtue, the spirit fails.
> Without spirituality, love fails.
> Without love, the world fails.
> The end!

Conversational Rape Example: Sweet Talk

Conversation:
Bill: I'm going to take you out this weekend and show you what a really good time is … Haha!
Mary: But, Bill, I already have a date.
Bill: Break it!
Mary: Okay, Bill. I'll do it for you.
Rape!

Rape Analysis

Bill exhibits the type of performance-oriented behavior common to Macho Super-Jocks. He is dominating, intimidating, insensitive, pushy, and grabby—any and all terms of this nature. In effect, however, Bill is probably very frightened, and his strategy to deal with these feelings is to overcompensate. Therefore, he steamrolls Mary. She is allowing herself to be conversationally raped into a Daisy Daffodil passive position because now she can say, "It's not my fault. He raped me."

Mary feigns helplessness when she says, "But Bill, but Bill," and Bill overrides her protests, giving Mary the excuse of having been socially raped because he is so pushy. In the eventual long-run scheme, however, Bill is the one who would be raped, because he would be responsible for Mary and her rape and the rape of the guy she was supposed to date in the first place. In blaming the whole situation on Bill, Mary can collect her angry stamps and continue her games with other men.

Straight Talk

Were this invitation effectively restated, Bill and Mary could conceivably talk as follows:

Rational Conversation:

Bill: Mary, I want to take you out this weekend if you're available.
Mary: I appreciate your invitation. But the fact is, I already have a date. Are you willing to ask me again?
Bill: Sure.

In the case of women relating to each other—and to men—some women control with passivity. As pointed out earlier, it is significant and important in an intimate relationship for a woman to respect a man. Since Bill has taken the risk of pursuing or reaching out to Mary, she has a choice. She can be helpless and passive, or she can be active, self-controlled, and responsible for herself. The latter choice disallows games.

By her sensitive responsiveness and consideration for his feelings, Mary rejects the invitation respectfully, promoting a willingness on Bill's part to reach out to her as a woman in the future.

Macho Super-Jock Bill tends to be very attractive to Daisy Daffodil Mary, in that Daisy is totally in charge of feelings, and Super-Jock is totally in charge of thinking. Between the two of them, they become one whole person. On the reverse side, Bertha Balls, the very performance-oriented woman, is very attracted to David Daffodil, a very passive-character man, in the same way that Macho and Daisy are attracted.

Relationships are based either on rational systems or emotional systems. If they're based on rational systems, then the man and woman complement, but do not replace, each other. In that way, the man brings a performance-process system, and the woman brings a process-performance system into the relationship. Both have permission to feel. They each have a separate responsibility to see that their particular side of the fence is in good repair. The man is in charge of problem solving, and the woman is in charge of the feeling level. In this way, no performance is done that might cause her significant pain and eventually reflect negatively on his performance.

Here is another sweet talk conversation.
Conversation:
Alice (on their third date): And Joe, it's okay if you spend the night rather than drive home.
Joe: Sounds nice, Alice, but where do I sleep?
Alice: Wherever you want.
Rape!

Rape Analysis

Alice is a pursuer, a performance-oriented female. She needed stroking and has opted to use the male system of dynamic pursuit over the female system of magnetic attraction to obtain those strokes. In her undercover message, which she has conveyed at the lower game level, she is inviting Joe to play with her sexually. Many women allow the intimacy of intercourse when what they really want are strokes of friendly affection—tender loving care (TLC). One of the big promotional abuses in the world today is telling women that they can experience intimate intercourse indiscriminately without hurting themselves. Since women are feel- thinkers and need to be safe and trusting for true sexual surrender, a woman who either invites or allows fast sex runs the risk of desensitizing herself to a total orgasmic experience.

In this dialogue, Bertha Balls Alice is herself being raped of her rights to be a woman. She's not allowing herself to be sensitive, to move slowly, or to be courted and pursued by a risk-taking male who knows how to solve problems, knows what he wants, and goes after it. Our friend, passive David Daffodil Joe, is now in the magnificent power position of receiving all of this deep generosity promoted by Bertha. Sadly, Bertha is really promoting Daffodil Joe's passivity. Also, Joe's negative attitude toward women as objects, things to use and play with, is being promoted.

Straight Talk

It is my experience that men want to solve problems, so that they can feel very, very self-reliant. They want to feel in charge, in control, and responsible when they do the performance pursuing. When Joe is pursued, he does not go through the process of problem solving. Therefore, he is actually at the mercy of Alice, which in effect undermines his masculinity and promotes his negativity. Because he feels this lack of control, he subconsciously distrusts her and will, in effect, use her, abuse her, and then ultimately leave her for another woman.

In this new choice, Joe will feel comfortable entrusting his feelings to a woman who loves herself more than Alice does, whom he can consider a worthy trustee of his own love feelings. Falling in love takes time and effort, but the value is more enduring.

Relationships are constructed on two different systems. One system is very definitely protective, the friendship foundation system. It protects the sensitivities of both parties and also allows the rational experience of the two elements of compatibility and communication.

The other system is based on chemical communication between two sensuous people who are more interested in *thing* body strokes than in spiritual love, sharing, and care strokes. As long as both people want the same thing, they will be okay. The risk comes when one wants love strokes and the other wants lust.

People often go to bed in order to eliminate intimacy, because true intimacy carries risk-taking pain. The massive modern fascination with sexual-chemistry relationships places compatible communication second. Relationships based on friendship place compatibility and communication first and chemistry second. Eventually, if the chemistry is there, the inherent negotiation of compatibility and communication will allow the sexual experience in a safe, loving way.

In consideration of the male, all too often today's man is being promoted to perform sexually. They end up with all kinds of sexual dysfunction that they've never had before. As I said before, when a man solves his problems, he feels more potent, and he's correspondingly more sexually potent as well. He is in charge of the situation, and when he's in charge of the situation and behavior, then the female part of him feels safe. When a man pursues a woman and he pursues her by being a trustworthy, honorable person, then he can, in effect, relax and enjoy himself.

A man who has been seduced and manipulated by his woman into thinking he's responsible for giving her orgasms, however, is a raped man. His problem will be manifested variably, from premature ejaculation to seminal retention, to impotence. The job is not performed because he knows subconsciously he shouldn't perform it. The accomplishment is not good for him as a man. Don't blame yourself because you didn't get the job done.

For example, in terms of the premature ejaculator, you're saying that you had better get your compatibility, friendship, and love factors lined up, because the chemistry is being damaged.

Seminal retainers are hanging on. You're really saying that you don't want to surrender. You don't want to give, because there is something inappropriate about the person you are with, or it may be that you have still not resolved your fear of demanding, taking women. Psychologically, the mostly easily understood sexual dysfunction is impotence. Impotence is saying, "I won't do it. And you can't make me do it, Lady."

Men, since they are very much interested in performance, are in charge of the concrete world. They see a pretty body; they want to touch it. That is very concrete. Women, on the other hand, are in charge of the abstract, spiritual world; they, in fact, are very much into not being touched unless they feel safe.

So, when a man sees a pretty girl, he responds to her concretely. When a woman sees a man, she thinks about his likability, his lovability. When two needy people relate to each other, we say they are symbiotic or parasitic. They need each other to fulfill themselves. Healthy people want each other, but do not need each other. I say that people come in two varieties—one shouldering the question "Who am I?" and the other directly an *I*, i.e., "I am myself, and I know who I am."

Symbiotic people simply do not share. They give or they take, but they do not share. One is a giver and the other a taker. In a sharing relationship, there is also give and take. They ask for and refuse from time to time. Importantly, however, in a sharing relationship, each individual predominantly takes care of himself or herself first.

Independent people are internally secure. Their childhoods were stable and they now feel well-loved by people. When they seek intimacy, they do so with the capacity to share that love with other people. The person who is not internally secure is anxious, constantly looking for love and a safe environment. When they find what they think they are looking for, they latch on, creating a mutually needy dependent relationship. Both lose, as both people continue to promote a lack of independence or *I*-centeredness.

Rational Conversation:

Alice: Joe, I enjoyed our date tonight, and I don't want to feel afraid for your safety. Will you be careful when you drive home?
Joe: It was nice, Alice, and I'll be careful. When can I see you again?

Conversational Rape Example: 'Til Death Do Us Part

Conversation:
Bill or Alice: Why don't you _____?
Joe or Mary: I can't, because _____.
Rape!

Rape Analysis

Again, we are viewing Macho Super-Jock Bill, Bertha Balls Alice, and their counterparts—David Daffodil and Daisy Daffodil Mary. All are intent on conversationally raping each other, just like Mom and Dad did to them when they were little.

Macho Bill and Bertha Balls Alice believe that action is more powerful than inaction, but they are mistaken. Daffodil Mary and Daffodil Joe can sidestep with their helpless, passive aggressive games until Bertha and Macho are themselves victims of both frustration and resentment.

When Macho and Bertha finally catch on to the rape and stop trying to get control of the relationship through power plays, they find that their Daffodil opposites take up the game and begin pressuring them in a role reversal. People who use active power are actually more afraid than the powerless passive partner who is safe enough to sit back and watch the fireworks. Remember, it is the one-down victim who actually gets the strokes from others—sympathy, pity, empathy, and rescuing. Bertha and Macho usually get left alone, looked down on, undermined in this scenario as the B-movie bad guys.

Marriage or committed one-to-one relationships built on a one-up, one-down system contain two question mark people. They are two humans, each of whom needs to trigger a rape in order to get a painful reaction like they remember from home.

Symbiotic, parasitic marriages can function indefinitely as long as no one moves out of line. If Bertha or Macho break down or Daisy or David build up, then a domino effect takes place that influences the whole family, including relatives who do not live with them. This can be a very good thing in a marriage, but often it ignites escape mechanisms like overeating, excess drinking, or extramarital non-negotiated affairs. If the changing people are open and honest, they can adjust to the new equality of "I'm okay and so are you." Professional help may be needed during this transition.

Straight Talk

In a good, balanced relationship, both people exhibit all varieties of behavior appropriately in response to all types of behavior in their partners. If a man cherishes his woman's feelings, he will listen to her without judgment and support her not-wants and general wants as much as he can, as long as they are moral, ethical, and legal. If a woman respects her man's thinking, she will listen to his specific wants and not-wants and respond to them as much as she can, as long as they are moral, ethical, and legal. Together they complement each other, and individually they grow and prosper. As they become more I-centered, they have more to share as a *we* couple and as an *us* couple in society.

This free exchange regarding individual wants and not-wants is handled by verbal negotiation.

In any committed relationship, there are four areas of negotiation: time, space, play (non-sexual and sexual), and money.

The first area of negotiation, time, comprises three subdivisions: time alone as an *I*, time together as a *we*, and time as a couple in relation to other persons as *us*. Healthy individuals make certain that they negotiate all three categories appropriately, i.e., I, we, and us. They maintain a balance among the three areas, being careful to avoid gamey rape deals wherein they intimidate or seduce each other out of balance.

Symbiotic couples over depend on each other as a *we*. Their alone time as well as their socializing with outsiders is reduced as they exhibit a pathetic need to hang on to each other, just as they did with Mommy and Daddy before they were five years old.

Individuals who are still fixated at an early level of growth usually believe that with good performance, they can earn love.

The contrary is true: you can never earn love conditionally.

By its very nature, true love is unconditional and only mature I-centered individuals can truly share it by accepting each other as is and being willing to negotiate without resorting to the tactics of intimidation or seduction.

The second area of negotiation is personal space, how it is shared and how it is cared for. We live in a possessive-pronoun world—my closet, your drawer, our dishes, my chores, and your chores. One of the first words a child learns is *mine*, and we carry the concept of ownership into adulthood with amazing tenacity. Too often symbiotic couples wrongly believe everything belongs to *we*, and then a rape situation occurs in which private ownership and a blurring of responsibilities takes place, which only promotes games and brings both pain and a breakdown of intimacy. To know where lines have been drawn is to establish stability, forestall misunderstandings, and promote closeness.

The third and fourth areas of negotiation are sex and money, respectively. Their inherent lines of responsibility draw perimeters around our two biggest areas of conversational rape.

Few couples have only physical sex problems. Most sex dysfunction is based on communication difficulties. Symbiotic, needy, question-mark people usually attempt to intimidate or seduce each other into a possessive, obsessive relationship. They disallow any space between them for such things as friendships with the opposite sex or a social life with same-sex friends. They very often become more needy and dependent, since no one person can fully satisfy the stroke hunger in another person.

A well-negotiated couple, on the other hand, allows for social interaction, even flirting—as long as it's kept within clearly couple-established guidelines. These include sexual exclusivity, and the knowledge that a comfortable, free person will feel more inclined to respond to an accepting, non-demanding partner than a punitive, controlling partner.

In the area of money, the power rape games come out in full force. Money has a spiritual power even greater than that of sex. Whoever controls the purse strings controls the relationship's health. The most balanced negotiation is to create clearly defined categories of *my* money, *your* money, and *our* money.

In this system, even when there is only one income, a portion is given to the non-paid partner to do as he or she pleases. It is disastrous for one or the other of the couple to ask for pin money. It automatically establishes a conversational rape situation. One person may be the designated bookkeeper; he or she may write the checks, keep the business details straight, and balance the budget, but that person benefits more by sharing the decision responsibilities with the other.

I want to summarize a statement about children relative to the four areas of couple negotiation—time, space, sex, and money. In these areas, children can share the negotiation during family council time (talking). But remember, the primary responsibility for setting up a good communication system is between husband and wife. Any time children outrank a husband or wife, trouble occurs. A man and a woman may not totally agree with each other, but they negotiate between themselves about the rules of the house—the dos and the don'ts, the wants and not-wants—before bringing the children into the transaction. When they arrive at a good negotiated compromise, they support each other in front of the kids in order to establish secure, stable guidelines for the marriage and for the family.

The purpose in all this negotiation is to establish clearly defined guidelines for the direction and goals of the relationship. In the absence of preplanning, the only alternative is spontaneous decision-making. And total spontaneity invites chaos.

In contrast, self-discipline makes room for occasional spontaneous activity, by creating an atmosphere of knowledgeable security in which it is safe to experiment. Both adults and children feel safer knowing where they stand in relationship to each other. With continuing open conversations, any couple can maintain a flowing, free, fun relationship. They can teach their children by example to avoid power games of intimidation or seduction. And they can teach their children to avoid the conversational rape of others.

I am a therapist, not a moralist. We all have a right do as we wish as long as we are willing to pay the price of those words and actions. The below are some of the most frequent questions I get with my responses.

1. Your significant other flirts for attention.

There are three ways to deal with people:

a. Accept them as they are even when you don't approve of them or their behavior.
b. Reject them in a loving, honest way.
c. Tolerate them, which means sometimes you accept and love them, and other times you disapprove and dislike them and their actions.

Children and adults can learn to handle consistent acceptance and love *or* consistent disapproval and dislike, but inconsistent acceptance and approval is crazy-making. One effect of addictive behavior is inconsistency. When a man is sober, he generally thinks clearly, grounded in his feminine, nurturing anima soul. When a man is practicing any addiction, he goes inside out and upside down into his feminine emotional need for sex gratification at the expense of those around him, especially his girlfriend, wife, or children.

When a woman is sober, she generally grounds her actions in sensitive feelings, which allow her to be open, receptive, available, and respecting—knowing she can always say no from her masculine animus soul should anything occur around her and her children that is immoral, unethical, or illegal.

When a woman is practicing *any* addiction, she goes inside out and upside down into her masculine emotional need to control the situation and all the people around her, especially her boyfriend, fiancé, husband, and son. Inconsistency hurts self-esteem in self and those he/she loves most, for they are vulnerable when in love.

2. Your significant other does not want as much lovemaking as you do. What do you do?

Unless your commitment to each other is an open relationship supporting sex with outsiders, you are non-committable and unable to negotiate a loving relationship. Once again, I am not a moralist; I am a therapist. If you as a couple negotiate ménages, swinging, and open sex—and you both accept and approve—I am not of a mind to impose my morality or ethics onto your relationships. We will deal with this issue more in a later chapter.

As an aside, I want to say that my idea of marriage and mating includes alternative styles, such as gay relationships. My goal is to help people to love one another, not decide which people will love which people.

3. Your fiancé wants you to be the homemaker and move to his (or her) career location as a breadwinner.

Over the course of a relationship, you will negotiate various styles of relationships from convenient equality to codependent inequality to covenant equity. If you dig in your heels before you marry, you will never be willing to ebb and flow as needs arise. *Next* will become your favorite word and act—until you realize there is no longer a next and you are alone.

4. You need an emergency loan of $1,000.

To not be willing to ask anyone who loves you before you ask a bank bespeaks of pride and an unwillingness to allow others to give, protect, and cherish you. Whether you are a prideful man out of touch with your feminine need to be nurtured, or a prideful woman who is unwilling to see if the men will give to you, or you are afraid to be vulnerable to being indebted to a man who might play one-up games—this still points to egotistical masculine pride and an unwillingness to receive and share.

5. You are engaged to a man/woman who thinks you have never been married or had a child or been bankrupt or in jail or addicted or any other "shame-full" thing.

You must disclose morally significant things, such as illness, sexually transmitted diseases (STD), and genetic issues. You must disclose ethical issues, which could impact his/her financial safety, such as bankruptcy. You must disclose legal issues of citizenship, criminality, marriage, divorce, paternity, and maternity.

What do you not need to disclose? You don't need to reveal your private sexual life before him or her. Very few human beings (saints are exempt) can handle total honesty. I call it a *lie for love* by commission or omission. These white lies are tactful ways to avoid useless information that once said cannot be withdrawn. In a world of virgin births and virgin marriages, lying for love would be superfluous. In a world of mistakes, rapes, incest, drugs, drinking, eating, and gambling, discretion is the better part of valor.

The *amends* part of a twelve-step program states that to make amends that injure them or others (ourselves) is not good. It's better to not have a relationship with someone who can't handle total honesty than to burden them with it. It's self-destructive to be rigorously honest about painful issues that: (1) are in the past, (2) are in the future—maybe, (3) have no moral, ethical, physical, or legal ramifications for you or them, (4) lessen one's image to another (especially men about a woman's sexual virtue and integrity), or (5) lessen one's image to another (especially women about a man's financial virtue and integrity).

In addition to being self-destructive, rigorous honesty is often aimed at ruining the relationship in order to lower anxiety. This is a way to get away from intimacy by dumping guilt on them to elicit empathy or pity as a sick form of codependent intimacy.

Also, being rigorously honest, which is insensitive to the feelings of the other person, shows a lack of compassion. Mary Lou didn't want to date Harvey anymore. She wanted to date Bill. Saying "I want to date Bill" directly to Harvey would be rigorously honest and unloving. "I appreciate the time we have spent together, Harvey, but I don't see our relationship going toward marriage, and I want to marry. I want to begin dating other men, and I'm telling you before I do it. I don't want to use you or lead you on."

Saying it this way would not be rigorously honest, but it would be more compassionate. Social finesse and good manners call for each of us to help one another to remain intact as human beings. Charity is love, and it outranks honesty in my opinion.

6. Your significant other is more successful than you are.

The male ego that binges on competitive superiority is unbalanced. How many times has a smart loving woman been avoided or dumped by an egotistical competitive male when he found out about her success? How many times has a smart loving man been seduced by a gold-digging, predatory seductive woman when she found out about his success?

Being productive is a masculine energy; being lovable is feminine. We all ebb and flow between the two if we are healthy. It is a man's world of money, power, and privilege, *and* we are all masculine. It is a woman's universe of love, *and* we are all feminine—so sharing is good for every man and woman.

7. Your significant other is sexually shy.

When I get a remarried client sent by the "perfect" partner, I know what the problem is. Prideful narcissism. We are all at various stages of experience and have various types of temperaments. Going together for team building is the best way to go.

George suffered from premature ejaculation. Sarah, 39, was f-r-u-s-t-r-a-t-e-d. George was almost perfect for her. He was committed to work toward marriage. They were best friends (soul mates). She dreaded bedtime knowing he would be nervous and guilty. She came to see me, and I advised her to invite him into a counseling session. He came, and we talked openly about his nervous shyness, his premature ejaculation, and courses of medical as well as behavioral changes in their sex life.

Over a few months of talking and doing, George felt more secure, Sarah felt nurtured and supported, and things got better for them. Being a team, a couple, and talking about a problem, builds intimacy. Relationships grow on the bad days. Good days are the reward for working through the bad ones.

8. You and your fiancé both work and live together. He/she does not like housework.

The limbic primitive reptilian brain is two to four million years old and communicates through intimidating and seductive body language. The four techniques used are: (1) tones of voice: yelling, whining; (2) facial expressions, glaring, swearing; (3) postures of the body, such as turning away or looking down or up at people; and (4) gestures with fingers and hands.

Only the neo-cortical brain, which is only 44 million years old, uses words, signs, and symbols to speak and write. Negotiating is the highest and most human form of communication. Fighting is—for animals, men, and women—at their lowest level of communication.

9. Your significant other wants a fifty-fifty financial convenient relationship.

In every relationship, a value judgment must be made. "Is this relationship at least 51 percent valuable to me?" If the answer is yes, then you have determined that this man or woman has the non-negotiable items you require, and therefore everything else is negotiable. 50-50 is not immoral, unethical, or illegal, so what is the reason for refusing? If the 50-50 is a non-negotiable item, *leave the relationship*.

10. You travel a lot for work.

Lying for love has to do with irrelevant information that has no moral (sexual), ethical (things that cost money, like property or money damage) or legal connotations. Putting yourself out as *single* when you have a commitment and lying for ego gratification is a signal that you cannot love. The only way you know you love yourself or anyone else is by the commitments you are willing to make *and keep*!

11. Your significant other's employer has laid off him or her.

No favor goes unpunished. Charity is what we do for people who *cannot* do for themselves. Favors are what we do for people who can take care of themselves, but our ego needs to be needed and have them dependent on us. To quit yourself based on their problem is our codependency. To live through another human indicates a lack within ourselves.

Being an independent, individuated, self-actualizing human requires that each of us be an *I* before we are *we* or an *us*. Codependency relegates us to *zero* and being unable or unwilling to develop a self that can negotiate with integrity.

12. You and your significant other have little time after work to socialize or sexualize.

Whenever a person is out of integrity, they play games of intimidation and/or seduction. To ask for dates and sex in order to get credit for being loving—and really only putting the other person in the position of saying "No, thank you"—lacks negotiating virtue. In other words, saying *only* what you mean is loving.

PART 2

We-ness
Courting or Dating?
Mating or Marriage?

16

DECIDING WHAT YOU WANT
OR DON'T WANT

As I said in part 1, I-ness, you must first answer these questions:

1. Am I dating this woman or this man for today's pleasure? Or am I courting this woman or this man for today *and* tomorrow's pleasure?
2. Is my goal legal marriage or long-term mating?
3. Do I want to be in an equal convenient relationship *or* an equitable covenant?

In either style, convenient or covenant, the beginning of courting, not dating, is when both people decide how much independence they are willing to give up and also how much gratification they expect and assume and how fast they need it.

In a marriage of convenience, equality in sacrifice and personal gratification are the goals. "I wouldn't stay in this marriage if he didn't provide such a great life," Georgianna said in a session with me. Thirty-five and beautiful with well-dressed elegance, she was typical of a "convenient" wife. Her prenuptial agreement had been painfully difficult but resulted in a good guarantee of security if the marriage failed.

Romance was not the bedrock of her marriage. Money, power, and prestige attracted her to Larry more than sexual attraction. Larry, fifty, balding and a little out of shape, saw Georgianna, his second wife, as an attractive, bright, valuable partner as he reached his peak years. He, like Georgianna, wanted the good life, but he was never going to naively marry again without protecting himself from financial disaster in another divorce. If he lost his money or she became ill, this marriage would be tested seriously.

This style of mating, or marriage, is very functional before and after children.

The major temptation in this style of mating or marriage is infidelity. Georgianna was very tempted to have an affair with Richard, 38, an up-and-coming musician, but thought better of it. Having sex was not as rewarding as having financial security.

Larry, on the other hand, periodically succumbed to the seduction of "gold digger" women and gradually gave it up as his marriage proved to be more valuable and his guilt more painful.

Georgianna and Larry shared equally in their marriage; they were not a power couple. In a power coupling, both people—straight or gay—are independent financially and autonomous. They are narcissistic and want both respect and cherishing equally. They don't believe in sacrificing any of their individual rights to think and communicate their thoughts and feelings and express all their feelings spontaneously or act on their own behalf.

When confronted about their narcissism, they scream, "You are trying to control me! I have a right to be myself!" Power couples divorce repeatedly or practice serial monogamy.

The covenant mating or marriage is the most intimate and requires the most spiritual development. Two people—whether straight or gay—deliberately delegate authority to lead to one while the other deliberately sacrifices a lot of independence to follow. Patrick, forty-eight, a successful stockbroker with integrity, proposed to LeeAnn, thirty-eight, also a stockbroker at the same firm. Both wanted children but wanted to see those children raised carefully and religiously, by them and not by outsiders.

LeeAnn had built her successful career and had been careful not to waste career time falling in lust with men who did not want to marry or have children. Patrick sounded perfect to her, and she was more than willing to give up her career to raise kids. She knew she could go back after the youngest was at least in pre-school.

Their goal in marriage was to form a team or two-in-one-flesh relationship. They both were willing to support each other's individuality, while at the same time giving up their narcissistic, individuated rights to be both respected and cherished equitably. It was a careful decision for both Patrick and LeeAnn to choose to sacrifice some freedoms for the team goal: a close-knit family.

Patrick would assume more financial responsibilities, while LeeAnn would assume more homemaking and child-rearing responsibilities. He would be respected and thus feel cherished. She would be cherished and thus feel respected equitably. Equality was not their goal; equity was.

A covenant requires that one person, male or female, express feminine receptive energy grounded in his or her worthiness and desirability, while the partner expresses masculine energy grounded in his or her competence and adequacy.

The covenant couple negotiates a mutual interdependency and becomes a balanced team or unit in the world for a greater good: a family. Sexual gratification and financial wealth are not the spiritual goals of a covenant.

The three necessities are chemistry (physical lust), compatibility (like) of goals for the relationship, and ultimately communicating (love) verbally through negotiation and nonverbally through sexual and non-sexual affection.

Phil and Patrice wanted a covenant marriage, but after Jake was born a year earlier, Phil resorted to intimidation to get his sexual needs met, almost to the point of competing with Jake for his mom's attention. Patrice learned quickly that she could seduce Phil into doing what she wanted by giving him sexual favors. Loving negotiation no longer worked for them, until they came in to see me as their marriage deteriorated into a codependency.

A codependent mating or marriage feels like the best in the beginning three months, the perfect period. Mary Ann, thirty, needed to be needed and Louis, thirty, fulfilled her needs. They met at a mutual friend's birthday party and binged on each other daily. Engaged and married in less than a year, Louis did Mary Ann's bidding until she felt smothered by his eager helpfulness.

As she became more and more secure and less codependent, she also became less respectful and more inclined to go out with friends to get away from him, which in turn caused him to cling more. His anger and her guilt drove them to a seminar. They identified with my description of a codependent relationship. They saw how Louis had been absorbed into

Mary Ann's life. His need for emotional symbiotic security had invited Mary Ann to "take him over."

She was narcissistic, independent, and overly controlling, wanting her thoughts and feelings put up as number one. Louis' self-esteem was so low he allowed himself to be treated as a victim or martyr rather than a person. If either Mary Ann or Louis were to emerge from codependency, the relationship would fall apart. Mary Ann and Louis worked on their marriage. I advised Mary Ann to demonstrate her respect for Louis by negotiating their date nights, money, and chores.

If he codependently didn't feel good about what she was doing, he could decide the price he would make her pay, such as divorce, separation, pouting, depression, or illness. By being two individuals, they set out their boundaries until they had a relationship of equity.

There are three ways to relate to another person:

1. You can accept him/her which means that you may not always like or approve of what they are and do, but you find more assets than liabilities, so you stay and work things out. To accept another person is to love that person, even when you don't approve of his or her behavior. If you like more about them than you don't like, help them and work it through. Mutate; don't eliminate. If you find someone who is at least 51 percent valuable on the *worst* day, keep that person.

2. You can reject anyone for any reason you have. I usually recommend immorality (body damage), unethical (property and money damage), and illegal (civil damage of your rights as a citizen). We all have issues we could improve on. Humans grow best in loving, accepting relationships. Use the tools in this book to negotiate changes.

3. You can tolerate your significant other, which is to half accept (love) and half reject (hate) the other. It promotes mood swings, which are difficult for you both. To tolerate is the only destructive thing in a romance. When you tolerate lateness, sloppiness, being overweight, burps, expelling of gas, lying, selfishness, cheating,

cheapness or insensitivity, you hurt yourself by failing your own sense of virtue and integrity.

Tolerating is a codependent game practiced by narcissistically deprived men and women—zero on the narcissistic scale of one to ten—who must acquire a human being rather than be one. To acquire a broken human is like going to a swap meet to buy a cheap, secondhand item rather than spending the money to get a new one, because you are not worthy of a new, unbroken one. Narcissists of either sex tolerate others' imperfections from their place of perceived perfection.

To be around these people is to live under a microscope. They constantly teach, preach, criticize, and rebuild others to their standards. Of course they fail and move on. When they meet their match, another perfect narcissist, the war is on. So you have only two choices: to accept them as they are—as long as they have one or two of the non-negotiable items you require and are moral and ethical—or to reject them cleanly and kindly.

Don't try to retrain them through lectures, arguments, put-downs, or criticism. This only damages their image of you as a sensitive, receptive, accepting woman, and does little good. Don't try to rebuild them. When you do, you're acting like a mother, and you're using masculine energy. If you get the job done, he becomes your feminine energy man, and you lose respect for him, while he gains respect for you at the cost of cherishing you.

Whatever you find missing in him, you can get from other sources. If he isn't crazy about ballet, go with a girlfriend or relative. If he doesn't have a jacket you like, give him one for Christmas or his birthday.

When people are loved and accepted, they hear what you're saying and choose either to modify their behavior or to pay the price of rejection by you. When you criticize or hassle people, you're being righteous and judgmental, and you're exhibiting your dark side.

Rachel, an anchorwoman for a local TV show, disliked the fact that her husband Ron, a developer, would plan things for them to do without consulting her. I suggested she say, "Ron, you really do plan fun times for us, but I'm uncomfortable when you don't ask how I feel about your plans. If you don't check with me, I'll automatically say, 'No thank you.'" Ron was angry for a while, but he did modify his behavior.

Take a position and anchor yourself. This idea of accepting or rejecting rather than tolerating him and his imperfections is a big part of staying married. When you are committed and want to be married, you're like two people on a life raft in a turbulent sea. Each of you has one paddle, not two, and is rowing on one side of the raft, not both. You are dependent on each other for power and direction. Any excess power plays will cause the raft to go in circles. Balanced energy is the name of the marriage game.

I suggest you now commit to the relationship and do your best on your side of the equation. This way, on the bad days, instead of looking at the person, you look rather to the survival of the relationship. Say to yourself, *I must do my part, even when my partner doesn't.* Don't abort a relationship that has value. Stay until you cannot stay. You'll know when to leave, because you'll feel both empathetic and apathetic toward your mate. The spark and the angry feelings will be gone.

However, if your mate is not overall 51 percent valuable, you cannot stay with them and remain healthy. Being in a toxic relationship may be a sign of unconditional love, but it's also a sign that you love them more than yourself. That is a sign of mental illness.

Martyrs and victims always need a toxic relationship to feed their mental illness. They feel uncomfortable when they have pleasure or there are no fights to be in. They are unable or unwilling to learn to balance the unconditional acceptance aspect of love and the conditional approval aspect of like. You need both in a relationship to be in a health-producing situation, whether it's being married, working together, nursing children, or visiting your relatives.

Avoid toxic people. You can get sick and die early around them. I recommend reading *People of the Lie* by M. Scott Peck for more information.

Here's a pledge I often ask both women and men to make: "I promise, on my honor, never, will I commit to a finite, fallible human being. Instead, I will commit to the relationship with a finite, fallible human being. I will do my half, and I hope to God they do theirs."

17

KEEPING COMMITMENTS

A masculine energy husband or wife must keep his or her commitments to maintain your respect. Any sloppiness with commitments indicates that he or she doesn't cherish your feelings and wants his or her feelings cherished instead. Narcissistic people always want to be respected and cherished, so if they fail to make or keep commitments, they want their behavior to be accepted, not challenged. But a woman or man with such a person will soon stop feeling cherished and will quickly lose respect for them.

Of course, at the same time that you're watching to see how your masculine energy man or woman handles priorities, he or she is watching to see how you are handling yours. Do you look appealing? Are you taking care of yourself? What about listening to his or her ideas? Are you fighting him or her for power and respect? Do you either break commitments or fail to make them? Do you fail to appreciate what they do to please you? Do you give *back* love, affection, time, and sensuous sexuality?

To get what you want as a cherishable man or woman, you must give your masculine husband or wife what he or she wants —unless it's immoral, unethical, or illegal. What about maintaining your primary role? Are you staying in your feminine receptive energy, or, if you are the masculine energy woman or man, the leader respected role? Often both people find that, after the period of bliss, their natural tendencies, drives, and behaviors start pushing them back into single narcissism.

Not every committed man or woman wants what is necessary to be *either* the feminine energy or the masculine. It can be very difficult to suppress a need to control and instead be passive, patient, and vulnerable. Also, it can be very difficult to suppress the urge to kick back and relax leadership in favor of waiting passive-aggressively if you are a tired masculine man or woman. Remember, complements attract, and similars repel.

Here's a pledge that I ask masculine energy women and men to take: "I promise, on my honor, to cherish women, kids, animals, and the planet, even when they are irrational, illogical, and often irritating."

Also, here's the pledge of feminine energy men and women: "I promise, on my honor, to respect my chosen man or woman and their thoughts, suggestions, ideas and plans, even when I know I'm smarter and can do it better, as long as they are moral, ethical, and legal. Furthermore, I promise to keep my yang mouth shut unless I have to call a cop, a doctor or a lawyer *first.*"

18

COMPATIBILITY

You and your mate (straight or gay) must be compatible, but that doesn't mean that you are clones. On the contrary, it's best if one of you has greater assets in the sexual, physical, playful, *oxygen* area and the other in the mental, thinking area of pragmatic things like money, property, bills, insurance, and groceries. Masculine energy men and women are *of* the world. Feminine energy women and men are *in* the world to make it fun.

Masculine people are the solid bricks, while feminine people are the pretty flowers. Bricks can be boring without flowers, and flowers are unprotected without brick walls and roofs.

Compatibility involves harmonies, morals and ethics, communication skills, and life direction—all the things that make a good friendship as well as a loving, romantic relationship. Compatibility is a matter of how much you enjoy the same things and what your goals are. It's a matter of whether you like the way they dress, the way they act in social groups, the way they eat and drink and their smoking habits, along with their religious choices, politics, ethics, financial assets, and educational background.

It's a matter of even more practical things, such as whether one of you is a morning person and the other is a night person. Snoring may be one of the biggest compatibility factors I have seen in my practice.

Compatibility has its non-negotiable and negotiable aspects. These need to be dealt with during the courting stage, before sex, because people who have sex too soon tend to think they're more compatible even when they aren't. They believe that love (sex) is all they need. Often they get married, but when the honeymoon period of about three months is over, reality hits, and the two people are faced with each other's defects. It's at this point that these couples become bored.

If I want to be married legally, in a covenant marriage of equitability, do I want to be the breadwinning masculine energy person who is responsible for the practical worldly issues of money? If so, am I comfortable sacrificing a lot of self-gratification for the marriage and family?

Or do I want to be the homemaking feminine energy person who is responsible for the quality of life and the sensual sexual love in the relationship and family? If so, am I comfortable sacrificing a lot of independent control over my own worldly life for the marriage and family?

When a convenient or covenant relationship fails, it becomes a codependency in which one person is totally responsible for the world of money and the quality of love, while the other clings like a child to a parent. As long as both parties are comfortable, all three styles work; the convenient equal, the covenant equitable, and the codependent inequitable and unequal. Every relationship fits into one or another categories—parent to child, child to parent, friends, and lastly, lovers.

Each style has three basic components. The first of these is chemistry-pheromone attraction between humans, which cannot be trained into anyone. When we have chemistry, we like to taste, touch, smell, see, and hear the other. When we don't have chemistry, we avoid the other even when they are family.

The second component is compatibility—a likeness of intellect, lifestyles, morals, and ethics. Great dissimilarities cause chasms between humans even in families. Similarities bring people together, at least intellectually.

Lastly, the third component is communication—either body and/or intellectual—symbolic. Talking and touching are the two basic forms of communication.

19

BUILDING AN EROTIC RELATIONSHIP

Sexuality is the most significant difference between healthy child to parent, parent to child, friends, and lovers. In the erotic relationship, all other relationship styles also exist—child-parent, friends, and ultimately, lovers.

I believe that relationships evolve in three-month cycles like seasons of the year.

Phases of a Relationship

As I have said, the first thing you must do is choose to be either the masculine giving, protecting, cherishing energy or the feminine receptive, available, respecting energy that gives *back* to the giver. If you want to be both, find a similarly narcissistic man or woman or find a *zero* who will be your submissive "slave."

A successful relationship has three components: chemistry, compatibility, and communication. Chemistry is lust, that attraction to one another. You can't do much about chemistry. You're either attracted to someone or you're not. Men especially need to *see* a sexually desirable woman or man. Women often need to *hear* a successful desirable man or woman. The major organ for a masculine energy man or woman is the eyes. He or she wants sex more than security. The major sex organ for a feminine energy woman or man is the ears. She or he wants financial status and security more than sexual pleasure.

Compatibility is how much you both like each other, and that often involves sharing common interests, enjoying the same things, and having the same goals.

Communication includes verbal as well as emotional communication, sex and affection, as well as spiritual communication. Communication and negotiation skills are the keys to intimacy in any situation.

When problems arise in communication, verbal negotiations and intimacy fail and give way to primitive old-brain intimidation and seduction, nonverbal tones of voice, facial expressions, gestures (the bird), and body postures. These cannot be negotiated, because they are winner-loser power plays. Only words can negotiate potency in a win-win communication.

I have found that in relationships, a crisis erupts every three months or so that spins the relationship significantly forward or backward.

1. The perfect phase: If this phase were a season, it would be summer, when you feel warm and malleable to each other. The chemical attraction is strong between the two of you. You both look right to one another, dress right, talk right, and your manners are correct. Everything is perfect.

2. The imperfect phase: This phase occurs usually right after a perfect phase, like autumn. People who have any fear of vulnerable intimacy usually like to abort the relationship during this period. Chemistry goes away and everything seems wrong. You're messy, ugly, and stupid.

3. The negotiable phase: The two of you face the winter cold, hard facts about each other, and you decide whether or not you are 51 percent valuable, worthy, and deserving of a chance to negotiate a compromise. Usually the four areas of negotiation are:

a. Money: mine, yours, ours. How do we handle it, and who does the handling?

b. Space: Should we move? How do we handle big maintenance items and chores between us? I recommend not living together unless engaged or married.

c. Time: My time without you, your time without me, our time together without *them*, and our time with *them*. What activities do we want to participate in, and which do we *not* want to participate in? Flexibility in role behavior is the best mode. Alternating masculine leader roles for feminine follower often helps the relationship to balance energy.

    d.   Play: This includes sexual and non-sexual activities. When filling this one out, it starts with "I don't want you to …"

Each person writes up his or her design for these four areas, and both come together to negotiate and compromise for best results. If necessary, hire a cognitive behavioral therapist to mediate without interjecting the person's moral ethical code into your plans. If you both wish to see a religious therapist, that's fine.

The commitment phase is like a new spring. This period provides new life to the relationship and forms a new, more solid foundation, for extended permanence. Nietzsche said, "If it doesn't kill you, it will strengthen you."

Never, never, never commit to a finite, fallible human being. Always, always, always commit to the *relationship* with a finite, fallible human being. Do your half of the commitment and *pray* they do theirs. Never project trust on a human being who can go wrong at any time for any reason. Instead, take a calculated *risk* on a 51 percent lovable human being, knowing you have faith that you can get help if things go sour.

With that, here is your pledge: "I promise on my honor, never will I commit to a finite, fallible human being. Instead, I'll commit to the relationship with a finite, fallible human being. I'll do my half, and I hope to God they do theirs."

Build a trustworthy record over the years, and if someone fails, start over with a new trustworthy record, *unless* violence (sexual or non-sexual) occurs or you are getting chronically ill dealing with the person. Stay in your committed negotiated marriage or mating until you get the lesson for you.

Some men and women stay and stay and stay because they want to do the right thing, but they get bogged down in guilt. For two years, Kathy had worked to save her troubled marriage to Don. Don half-heartedly participated with her in counseling sessions, but nothing ever gelled. Kathy finally was ready to leave, but Don tearfully clung to her, promising changes. She left, but felt guilty for causing him so much pain. She asked me how best to deal with her guilty feelings.

What did I do? Emotional apathy and empathy for the other are signs that you have the lesson. He or she who stays to the end goes to the next higher level. He or she who leaves early repeats the lesson until learned.

I told her, "The reason you're ending your marriage after two years of work probably is because you care so much about how *he* feels. Apparently you want a man you can both respect as a husband and cherish as a boy. The only man who needs to be respected and cherished is a narcissist. The lesson you need to learn is that you cannot be a doormat 'zero.' My guess is that as you attempt to divorce him, he'll snap to and start performing exactly as you want him to—respectfully.

If by this time you've de-bonded and fallen out of love with him, you won't see his recovery as authentic, but it is. A man who has been spoiled by a mothering, narcissistically deprived woman resents her, because he knows she doesn't respect his ability to handle pain and solve problems as a man. Now that you're planning to cause him pain by leaving him, he'll finally feel rejected by you and start cleaning up his Peter Pan act."

Another client, Lucille, gained forty pounds after two kids, and Guy was turned off sexually. He offered to send her to weight loss clinics and offered wardrobe incentives, but nothing worked. She enjoyed being a mom so much that she neglected Guy's needs to be with a sexually healthy desirable wife. He was sorely tempted to have an affair with Marilyn at the office but didn't. In desperation, he moved into the guest bedroom. Lucille was shocked.

She had believed her mother when she had said that Catholic marriages stay together no matter what. Lucille knew her mom, Harriet, neglected her husband, Lucille's dad George, and turned her eyes away from George's affairs. "Men always are unfaithful; you put up with it for the children's sake." Lucille's lesson was painful but she got it. She had forgotten that Guy had a right to expect equity. He worked hard as a breadwinner, and he had a right to expect sensuous sexual gratification from his wife. She got her lesson, and the marriage flourished.

20

WHAT ABOUT SEX AND
SEXUAL DIFFERENCES?

If you're dating, sex is a natural part of the date. If you're courting, sex is the flower on the tree of life and love. All I need say about dating sex is: be safe. Don't trust any man or woman. Take only the risks you can afford. If you don't trust anyone and they prove untrustworthy, you will be safe. The words *risk* and *risk-taking* are more appropriate than trust.

Now as for courting—sexuality, science, and anatomy can guide us. Freud said, "Anatomy is destiny" and as time goes by we prove this correct.

Estrogen resides in every human being, male or female, but most often in pre-menopausal women (forty-five to sixty-five) and post-andropause (forty-five to sixty-five) men. Estrogen is an *affect* hormone. It cares more about the universe of feelings than the universe of thinking, which is more of the testosterone (men) and progesterone (women) arena. Estrogen does not want pain. Testosterone and progesterone can handle pain better.

Young men and older women want action, performance, and a concrete reality. *I want* or *I think* are yang masculine words. Young women and older men say *don't want* and *I feel*, which are yin feminine words. They want to make love, while young men and older women want to make money. Abstractness, processing, and receptivity are the feminine universe. Maleness, whether in a woman's body or a man's, calls for production and performance.

A man's body is built to perform. A woman's soul (yang-animus) is created to love and perform, to give, to nurture, to protect the young, the old, and the sick. When her soul goes instead for money, power, and prestige, she encounters a painful, worldly reality, which can stressfully imbalance her fertility chemistry and may lead to clinical depression. The proverbial *clock ticking* is today's harsh medical reality depriving women of children.

A man's yin soul (anima) longs for love, but not until he is off testosterone and older will he be able to halt his physical need to procreate and have sex for sex's sake. A woman's body is also built to perform but in a different way than a man's. Hers is built to be impregnated and then to give back a baby. Her body, unlike his, is *not* built to give, protect, and cherish people over ten and under sixty-five, especially sexually.

A woman's yang animus soul is created to give back performance love sexually when her body has been cherished and protected. Young women (premenopausal) need to feel good in their bodies to do spiritual loving good with their animus yang souls by saying no to casual sex for sex's sake.

A man's anima (yin) soul longs secretly and idealistically for spiritual love but not until he is going off testosterone (post andropause). Older men will be able to channel their *concupiscence's* penile thrust quotient needed to procreate and have sex for love's sake.

If a man has the fortunate misfortune of having money and animal magnetism (the alpha male), he will easily overwhelm a nice sweet beta girl, *or* he will find a challenging alpha woman (smart and beautiful) who will either give him casual sex until he is either addicted or bored and off to his next conquest, *or* she will say no and he will have the time to fall in love with her soul *before* he gets her body.

Too many women today narcissistically sell out sexually for money, power, and prestige, thus cutting a man's ability to fall in idealistic, spiritual love. I believe women, not men, are spiritually non-committable today.

Young men need to *do good* to *feel good*, and doing good is having sex with a desirable woman. Little do men know the price they pay when they have sex with a young woman who cannot say no because she too is male and wanting to perform and compete and conquer a successful man through sexual addiction (sex for sex's sake) and not love. Men beg for sex they know inside is wrong, and masculine women give in sexually when they know it's wrong.

Older men often feel better with younger women, and older women often do better with younger men. The problem with this is that having a second family for an older man is difficult, and not having a family at all for a younger man is difficult to reconcile in marriage or mating. Compatibility is important.

21

WHAT ABOUT BRAIN DIFFERENCES?

The brain has become a well-examined organ since the advent of Functional Magnetic Resonance Imagery (FMRI) and other scientific tools. Lateralizing the two brain lobes—yin right and yang left in men and women, straight or gay—has resulted in the knowledge that the left lobe, the yang, masculine thinking lobe in men and women, does the most teaching, verbalizing, problem solving, and solution giving.

The right lobe, the yin feminine feeling lobe does the most sensuous, nonverbal, sexual, and processing reception. Between the two lobes lies a connecting fibrous bridge called the corpus callosum that processes information from both lobes. It is bigger in women, left-handed men (like Einstein, Picasso, Da Vinci and Michelangelo) and anatomically gay men, which allows them to process thinking and feelings simultaneously. Right-handed men have a smaller connection and therefore they have a tendency to speak from either one lobe or the other, but not both at the same time.

Some sex differences in the brain arise genetically before a baby takes his or her first breath. People usually have forty-six chromosomes in each cell. Two of these chromosomes, known as X and Y, are called sex chromosomes, because they help determine whether a person will develop male or female sex characteristics. Girls and women typically have two X chromosomes, while boys and men usually have one X chromosome and one Y chromosome.

The X chromosome carries with it 1,200 genes, while the Y chromosome carries twenty-one additional genes. Females (what we all start out as) have two X chromosomes, for an XX set. Males have an X and a Y, for a XY set. One of these genes is known as the SRY gene, and it is the master switch that starts development of testes to turn the fetus into a male.

During the first six weeks of pregnancy, mother and baby cocreate the sexual identity of the baby hormonally, especially the XY boy. Every baby begins life duplicating mom's body: girl-girl (the XX chromosome). When the Y chromosome triggers a response in mom's body, baby and mom rebuild androgen resulting in some boys not getting enough, resulting in feminized brains and body (anatomically gay); some girls get too much androgen, resulting in masculinized brains and bodies.

Male hormones, testosterone, and vasopressin in men vary daily (high in the morning and low in the evening) and yearly (high in the autumn and low in the spring).

This difference of either getting enough or not can cause loving communication and negotiation problems. On the other hand, a left-handed man and a woman can end up so neurologically similar that they compete for thinking and feelings, which neutralizes energy.

A cortisone hyperplasic adrenalized female is neurologically similar to a male brain, resulting in the little girl fetus turning into a boy.

I spoke to a nice East Indian man some time ago, and he told me about an Indian practice of giving women herbs to support maleness in the fetus at forty-two days. While I am disappointed in the anti-female attitude, I am amazed at the scientific intuition of even thinking of influencing gender with herbs. The only problem is sometimes mom and baby don't correctly input the amount of more masculine, thinking, doing communication and behavior.

As I have said before, complementary systems attract intimacy, while similar systems repel. The neo-cortical brain can learn to use verbal and written language in a negotiable win-win style and avoid limbic-primitive animal level narcissistic gamey competition that only intimidates with fear or seduces with guilt in a win-lose style.

22

HOW DO WE COMMUNICATE INTIMATELY?

Narcissistic men and women want to be respected for their thinking and also cherished for their feelings. The only men and women they can relate to are of the same narcissistic style. They can negotiate a convenient equal relationship *or* they can fall into an inequitable codependency in which one person narcissistically intimidates while the other acts seductively helpless.

In each of these three types of relationships—convenient, codependent, and covenant— the straight or gay couple must pick its style. If one picks one style and the other another style, communication automatically breaks down, no matter how much chemistry or compatibility of lifestyle exists. A convenient relationship consists of two equal partners, both contributing financially, sexually, with chores, with responsibilities—and both wanting respect for performance and cherishing for processing love physically, mentally, and emotionally.

A codependency is a slave-master, parent-child relationship in which one person wants all the respect for his or her performance as leader-master while also wanting to process cherishing. It's a "Don't talk back or cause me pain" attitude. One is a ten; the other, a zero. I am not judgmental about people choosing this style. Some religions believe it is God's will, and it works because men and women transcend common sense for God's will until they are brought to spiritual consciousness about their individual rights to be respected and cherished as an individual before God.

The last style of relationship is the covenant. Each partner voluntarily sacrifices and disciplines himself or herself for the sake of the equity team. One person takes pride in taking on the yang leadership responsibility in the area of money, power, and prestige while the other yin energy person takes pride in releasing a great deal of independence to follow the yang sensually and sexually for an equitable exchange of yin/yang energy.

In a convenient, equal relationship competition *I think I want* or *I feel I don't want* neutralizes the chemistry ending up with a sexless relationship that can make lots of money but little love.

If a couple wants a good equal sharing convenient relationship, the two partners must remember to use language that is complimentary such as "I feel badly about_____; what do you 'think' about this solution and what do you want me to do to help?" *or* "I 'think' I want _____; how do you 'feel' about this?" and "What can I do to help you feel better?" Right lobe communication about feelings directed at left lobe logic is complementary, not competitive.

In today's equality, egalitarianism is best for all relationships in and out of the home and office. My office is full of equal moms and dads with their kids, equal employers and employees, equal friendships, equal marriage partners, and equal dates. Very few people remember that our country is a republic based on equity, not a democracy based on equality. We don't vote directly for the president, as we saw in the Florida fiasco in the election of 2000. We vote for our electoral college representatives. We sacrifice some of our individual equal rights for the sake of a more equitable system of law and order. I have found that spontaneity produces chaos, and discipline allows spontaneity.

Although I do believe that there are only two games in town involving money, power, and prestige—male (yang) and sexual and sensuous (female, yin) in this day and age, simultaneous careers of equal financial reward are common. Often the yin-feminine energy makes more money and has more power and prestige than the yang-masculine. How do two people make the covenant relationship work?

It can work by making sure that the two people flow with the energy exchange and don't trample one another. In other words, who is respected and who is cherished? Who is the active, giving yang masculine energy, and who is the passive yin, receptive, feminine energy?

Peter, an associate professor of history, made about half as much money as his girlfriend Paula, an advertising executive. However, Peter was clearly the "man" in the relationship and Paula admired and respected his position and intellect. As the cherished one, she brought sensuality into their lives together. When Peter went to Paula's apartment, he could relax. She provided a comfortable and loving environment.

After nine months of a mutually monogamous, long-term sexual relationship, Paula knew she wanted to marry Peter. She tingled when he told her decisively what he wanted, whether it was a date or making love. She needed her man to be the leader, and she responded to his leadership sexually and sensuously. She felt secure, and so did he.

Peter loved her vulnerability. It was a sexual turn-on for him to be in control of her pleasure with his body and mind. He felt her trust in him building, and because of their mutual trustworthiness, he could take more risks and be more creative about leading and pleasing her. She brought his masculinity out sexually and he brought out her sexual femininity. They married at one year, six months.

Being equal in career and brains doesn't mean being equal in energy preferences. Everyone has innate talents and preferences. One person genuinely likes to make reservations or pay bills, while the other likes to cook or prefers initiating sex. They can talk about preferences and talents and negotiate interdependency.

Beware of narcissistic men and women who—to keep painful distance between you—will neither talk about what they want nor about what they do not want. They are afraid of intimacy. Superficiality is their goal of non-commitability. Getting money and having sex are their real goals. Sharing feelings and not wants or thinking wants are the goals of truly lovable men and women.

Left lobe communication about ideas, wants, and suggestions directed at right lobe sensitivity is also complementary and not competitive. In a convenient relationship, both people are respectable breadwinners, and both people are cherishable homemakers, equally sharing money, sex, chores, and maintenance responsibilities. Periodically, they sit down and renegotiate time, space, money, play, needs, and wants to keep the relationship vital, alive, and intimate.

In a covenant relationship, one person is designated by both people as the respected "breadwinner" left lobe, masculine, yang partner whose thoughts and actions have a priority unless they are immoral, unethical, or illegal. The partner is designated by both people as the cherishable "homemaker" right lobe, feminine yin partner, whose feelings, physically and emotionally, have a priority unless they are using their feelings to control their partner into a codependent mommy or daddy role.

The thought of negotiating a way to communicate what you want (masculine yang) or what you don't want (yin feminine) turns people off, because they think it's too analytical, too businesslike, too unromantic, and too cold. But to me, negotiating for mutual benefit eliminates that horrible moment when you realize that the person you're in a covenant with is either an intimidator or a seducer who now wants your life, body, money, or spirit. You've been taken over by a narcissistic body snatcher.

However, if you use Amigo Talk (what is stated in the rest of this chapter and the next) early enough, you may avoid that moment and perhaps even sidestep the games or the game-playing person. You may not need to waste time recovering from the pain of another failed relationship. Negotiating in a complementary style is a skill that healthy men and women must have in order to be good covenant team members.

Emotions are different from feelings. A feeling flows from body sensations (gut feelings) through the rational brain and ends up in an appropriate action. Emotions burst out in irrational behavior such as yelling, throwing, hitting, or leaving. In extreme cases, murder and mayhem result, necessitating police intervention. Being emotional is reactive and chaotic. Being rational is proactive decision-making, choosing to speak and act in a predetermined way.

Just as we all become potty trained or else we cannot go to school, so too we all must train our speech and behavior, even when we are feeling emotional. Once you've done this, you can cut down the chaos and clear the way for smooth complementary energy communication. In a covenant relationship, surrendering some of your rights to be respected or cherished will facilitate your ability to work through problems with less conflict, competition, and confusion.

Disciplining your speech and not acting out is the sign of a mature adult.

I advise (and use as a pledge) the yin man or woman to never ask for more, better or different love, affection, time together or sex, because these must be freely given by the yang man or woman as "gifts," not obedient service. 51% valuable means enough time, enough sex, enough love and enough affection is being given to warrant staying in the relationship.

If you complain it is not enough, then be prepared to leave or be left with the following admonition: "I obviously do not give, protect, and cherish you enough. Therefore, I am going to free you to find someone else who pleases you more." Nagging will get you free but rarely get you what you want. Feminine yin women and men get what they want by knowing what they don't want. Masculine yang men and women get what they want by asking for it and caring how their partner feels about it.

You can occasionally switch roles. In a covenant relationship, switching from being the yang, masculine breadwinner respectable person into the yin, feminine homemaker, cherishable person only calls for permission. "Honey, I have some painful feelings to share with you about _____. When will you be comfortable, today hopefully (don't go to sleep unheard and unknown, it builds up a resentment and later blows up) to hear me out?"

or

"Honey, I have some ideas, wants, suggestions, and questions about _____. When will it be convenient, today hopefully, to hear me out?"

Whether in a convenient or covenant relationship—straight or gay—complementary communication lends itself to more intimacy than competitive communication.

23

How to Fight Rationally, Not Emotionally

As a California Licensed Marriage, Family and Child therapist, Certified Transactional Analyst (TA) and Certified Addiction Specialist in Alcoholism and Sexual Addictions, I wrote my doctoral dissertation on "Androgynous Semantic Realignment" (ASR) and later received a government service mark for it as WANT® Training. What you are reading and learning is a segment of this training, which focuses on negotiating with love using our brains left lobe.

Rational men and women are in touch with their thoughts and feelings before they speak or act. Emotional men and women are *not* in touch with either their thoughts or their feelings. An emotional, drunk, or drugged man will abandon his thinking logic in favor of his emotional, feminine reactive and sometimes violent feelings. To be rational and sensitive to those he loves, a man must feel his feelings, think, and ask himself, *What do I want?* and act on it through communication or direct physical action.

An emotional, drunk, or drugged woman will abandon her sensitive feelings in favor of controlling masculine thoughts. To be a rational and sensitive woman, she must ask herself, *What is it I do not want?* and act on it through communication or direct physical action.

There are three conflict tools, and they are:

1. Stroke and Stand—used immediately and in the moment.
2. Five-Step Clean-Up—used after the incident.
3. Validation—used to flush the emotional limbic intimidation and seductive game to the surface to be negotiated rationally.

There are four signs of a gamey emotional communication bent on either narcissistic self-gratification or control over you, otherwise known as a loser in communication. They are:

1. Evasiveness—"I will never negotiate details concerning time, amount, location, who was there, or what was said, so you cannot catch me in a broken agreement."
2. Secretiveness—"You must mind read my thoughts or feelings. I will not say what I want (masculine) or what I don't want (feminine). Therefore, you must do all the communication work like my mommy or daddy."
3. Condescension—"I am above you, one up, and can intimidate you with fear, or I am littler than you, one down, and can seduce you with guilt."
4. Abruptness—"I will not speak in full sentences, only single words or gestures. You will never know the details, so I can never be held accountable."

In a Stroke and Stand response, a man or woman senses the game being played in the body first, then responds with loving acceptance by saying that the significant other has a right to say, think, feel, do, or not do whatever he or she did. He or she need not approve of the statement, action, or lack of action; he or she needs to only acknowledge the freedom and innate rights of the other to do something that causes pain on any level.

Next, a choice must be made rationally and not emotionally to make either a masculine thinking statement and asking for a want *or* a rational, not emotional, feeling feminine statement stating what is painful and not wanted.

Lastly, a contract is proffered. "Will you or will you not _____?" If no rational answer or commitment is made, he or she must accept or reject this lack of negotiation. A price may or will be set that is small, medium, or a rejecting large one that may result in a termination of the relationship, depending on the seriousness of the emotional intimidation or seduction.

A Five-Step Clean-Up tool is used out of context. It is my version of a cold call in sales. An incident has occurred earlier but is not dealt with rationally (feel, think, and act), perhaps only emotionally (feel, react irrationally, and act).

Whenever a man or woman has a need to initiate a painful communication, it is best to get permission using complementary transactions. "I think … what do you feel?" *or* "I feel badly. What do you think?" "I have some pain, confusion about something you said or did earlier. When would it be convenient today (respecting their masculine thinking) or comfortable (cherishing their feminine feelings) to hear me out?" This could be followed by a Stroke and Stand statement along with a sensitive statement of painful feelings. If you feel the need to bring up an old painful situation out of context, always include your feelings, even if you are a man or masculine woman.

Never stay for more than two negotiations as a game of one-upmanship is being played. Two negotiation rounds means that instead of answering the question "What do you want and how can I help you and get it?" your partner defends, argues, questions, filibusters, vents emotions, or gets violent, verbally or physically, thus converting the negotiation into a gamey uproar of intimidation and seduction.

Uproar is pure emotions using tones, gestures, postures, and facial expressions along with irrational words to end all negotiation in which you might get some of your needs and wants met. Narcissists like the game of uproar.

Only saints can withstand more than two rounds of an emotional barrage. Humans do well to get out of the game before the emotional limbic animal nature erupts, sometimes in violent verbal degradation or even in physical violence. Young men especially are prone to outbursts of a physical type due to testosterone.

When dealing with a passive-aggressive man or woman, it is best for you to not try to get them to answer a question. Fill in the negative answer yourself. They obviously don't want to negotiate your needs but they don't want to openly say *no* to you hoping you mind read *yes* and go away, at least for now. If you do want to say something, use a Stroke and Stand. "You have every right to not answer my request with a straightforward yes or no, so I will fill in the blank with a no until you are willing to negotiate." This stops the game and hopefully allows a resolution to occur at a later time.

The last conflict tool is Validation. Ninety percent of all communication is nonverbal body language. Tones of voice, facial expressions, gestures, and body postures are perfect ways to use our primitive animal limbic nature to play games of intimidation and seduction. Only 10 percent of all communication uses verbal or written symbols.

In order to flush the nonverbal to the verbal, it is important to validate the nonverbal messages, i.e., "I believe or think or sense from your tone, facial expression, gestures, or postures that you are feeling mad, sad, etc. Am I right?" All answers other than yes or no are passive aggressive ways to avoid negotiating.

It is best for you to fill in the blank yourself with a Stroke and Stand statement. If your partner agrees with your statement about his or her negative feelings, then you can set up a time to communicate for resolution.

These three tools have carried my clients and me through painful, emotional, intimidating, and seductive games. Mutating (evolving?) rather than eliminating relationships is the best way to live and love. *Next* is a dirty four-letter word, unless violence or your illness requires your exit.

PART 3

Us-ness
Children and Parents

24

CONVERSATIONAL RAPE AT HOME

As a reminder, the term *rape* is ordinarily used in reference to the physical, sexual violation of another human being, but there are other kinds of rape that violate the mind and spirit of a human being in ways that may or may not leave physical marks. Jails and mental hospitals are full of people who bear no physical marks to show the rape that has taken place. I have termed this more subtle form of rape *conversational rape*.

All humans are born with the potential to feel through the body senses of taste, touch, smell, sight, and hearing. This oldest part of the brain, the reptilian or limbic brain, is two to four hundred million years old. Its forms of communication are facial expressions, gestures (today the *bird* says a lot), postures (especially used by teens), and tones of voice. The goals of this form of nonverbal communication are intimidation with fear and seduction with guilt. Gamey communicators use this form of communication to gain power over others.

Humans think symbolically through imagery and/or dreams and words. The neocortical brain or newer brain is only 44 million years old, but it is the negotiating brain, the win-win brain, and the intimacy-building non-gamey brain. Psychological stability, social interaction abilities, deductive and inductive reasoning, and problem-solving capabilities (IQ) are all determined by language abilities.

When this language training begins, before one year old and hopefully by eight months, sound and symbol are imprinted on a baby's brain. If an Asian baby does not hear non-Asian language before eight months—the sounds of *l* and *r*—it can never reproduce those sounds and vice versa. Today babies are physically signing before talking, because it's an easier form of communication for the brain to learn.

The motivation behind a baby's training will be based on one of two types of love. One is unconditional acceptance, love that recognizes the rights of the little child to have any and all feelings, wants and not wants, and to express them. The second restricts the child to "right" and "wrong" feelings, should and should nots. In this latter language program, conditional love is given (doled out) for good performance.

The child, in order to survive in the family unit, soon learns how to activate negative processes, games of intimidation based on fear, or games of seduction based on guilt. Whether suppression, repression, projection, sublimation, or compensation, these processes cloak the child's true feelings and thoughts, rather than allow for their free expression.

Through this language-training program, the personality and identity of the trainer parent, (stepparent, foster parent, nanny, au pair, or grandparent) and the trainee child bind together to perpetuate a system that systematically rapes both of their true feelings, thoughts, and free actions. It is more a reactive should/should not program than an action want/not want program. The resulting behavior has been labeled gamey, neurotic, and/or psychotic, which always includes physical damage.

Conditionally loved children have been psychologically raped by intimidation through fear of abandonment and/or rejection. The physically battered child is the ultimate gamey rape victim, but the nonphysical psychological rape perpetuated through language, both verbal and nonverbal, can be as violent to the mind and spirit as the physical rape is to the body.

If the basic language-training system were based on intimidation and seduction (i.e., "Do it or else I will not love you" or "Do it for me, and I will love you more"), the person will believe that this conditional love system is the right way to do it and will use the system on those surrounding him or her, thus perpetuating more intimidation and seduction, more conversational rape.

The purposes of this us-ness division of this book are as follows:

1. It shows the influence of language and communication systems on human beings from embryo to grave.
2. It demonstrates how humans are conversationally raped themselves and how they rape others.

3. It raises the reader's awareness and conveys new ideas on how to recognize intimidation and seduction in communication and thereby how to avoid the rape consequences.

4. It teaches the reader how to love himself or herself and others better, particularly little children, in order to make this a more loving world in which to live.

25

RAISING HEALTHY KIDS, A GLEAM IN DADDY'S EYE

Men see with their eyes, sex gratification, women hear with their ears sex gratification. Gratification stimulates the five senses: taste, touch, smell, sight and hearing. Casual intercourse sex is gratifying, but also less satisfying. Gratification is hedonistic, while satisfaction is stoic. Men under age fifty generally want gratification sex even if it is not as satisfying long term. Women under fifty generally want satisfying love making even if it is not totally gratifying, so long as status and financial support are satisfying.

A future daddy sees his wife physically and approaches her for either intercourse or to make love. A future mommy either hears his request or feels his touch and says yes or no to sex, especially if she feels grateful for his generosity and protective financial behavior.

The baby is conceived either way through casual hedonistic sex or stoic making love. How does the baby grow in the womb? All embryos are XX female chromosomes or XY male for one week. When mommy identifies the Y chromosome, she releases the master SRY gene and the male Y baby starts to develop testes and produces testosterone.

By 26 weeks of gestation, the body and brain of the XY boy are observable on a scan. Each person can be genetically and hormonally one of the below.

- clearly male;
- clearly female; or
- anywhere on the continuum between male and female, which may cause transsexualism (gay or lesbian)

Conversational Rape Example: A Gleam in Daddy's Eye

Expectant mom: I hate being pregnant!
Expectant dad: You were the one who said you couldn't get pregnant.
Expectant mom: Why is everything always my fault?
Rape!

Rape Analysis

Here is a case of a man and a woman engaged in conversational rape because of anger and guilt. She is complaining about being a pregnant victim of a man. He is attempting to alleviate his guilt by dumping the responsibility back on her. The circle of strife continues; she gets hostile and defensive.

Conversational rape is a combination of seduction and intimidation, with these people manipulating, in a gamey way, for both power and strokes.

The real victim in this rape is the unborn child living within the anxious, cortisol-adrenalized body of the woman. Luckily, cortisol does not cross the placental barrier.

It is this little human who receives the true messages of negativity passing through mother. Baby perceives and thinks in pure sensations of pain and pleasure, without the benefit of thinking symbolically with words or images. Baby records these negative perceptions on his/her neurological system as the foundation of his/her reality.

Should this negative behavior continue, such a pain-centered human may become a pain addict. Comfort will be available only with the experience of physical, mental, or emotional pain. Discomfort will arrive whenever too much pleasure is apparent.

On the other hand, a baby may grow into a person who chooses to become a no-pain addict. This person continually avoids pain as if it could kill him or her. However, no-pain addicts are anxious to stuff or suppress their pain and may drink excessively, overeat, or indulge in drugs or sex. Believing they are escaping destruction, they are in reality promoting it.

When we lose pleasure significantly at birth, we then become mistrusting of pleasure. We become more aware of feelings, deciding it to be an unreliable system, and move up into our heads—thinking. Such people actually become pain-centered. Pain is polarized, and they gravitate from one extreme or the other—toward pain or away from it.

The parent-centered home seeks retribution for the parent, and the baby is forced to live in that environment. The parents have deprived feelings, and they resent the baby's interference with their need for strokes to counter that deprivation.

In a child-centered home, the parents have been at one time well-gratified children. Therefore they pass this on to their babies, and their babies are well-gratified. By generously touching, by generously loving, by feelings that surround the baby, by the vibes, and by responding to the baby's needs, the baby's feelings receive priority.

Straight Talk

Straight talk in this situation would involve the mommy and daddy in a search for ways to gratify each other, in order for them to give generously to the baby. Then the baby would naturally learn to turn this feeling back and the positive energies generated form a complete circle in the cycle.

The first solution for this situation is for Mother to embark on a good prenatal program. Physically, she makes certain that her body is well-loved and nurtured. She is careful about nutrition, exercise, and weight. Mentally, she controls her environment in comfortable ways. This will help her deal with problems as they arise. Her mind should continually nurture her, reminding her to mother herself and receive mothering through her mental processes.

Mother's mind will not trigger anxiety if she receives the support she needs in her environment. Emotionally, the mother sees to it that she experiences a maximum of pleasure, because the anxious body has a tendency to put out toxic chemicals that have a very negative effect on the nervous system.

The nervous system is the communication center between a mother's body and her baby's body. What Mother puts out in the way of neurological messages will be sent to that baby. Good prenatal programs—physical, mental, and emotional—are of paramount importance for the child.

Also, Mother should receive a childbirth system in which the mother and the baby work together in a pleasure-centered way to the greatest degree possible, so that the baby maximizes the pleasurable experience of the birth process.

Measurement of the birth process in terms of pain and/or pleasure has much to do with mother's anxiety level. Being educated in the birth process and feeling good about the process taking place both help the expectant mother relax her body enough to provide the most pleasure-centered transition phase for the baby, going from the uteral to postpartum state.

Birth Without Violence, provides a poignant statement about a pleasure-centered birth process. For an awareness of the extreme damage that can be done, Arthur Janov's book, *The Primal Scream* is a statement of concern over the physical, mental, and emotional trauma of birth.

After a good prenatal program and a sensitive birth system, a baby is launched into the world. As Dr. Leboyer outlines, it is of extreme importance that skin-to-skin contact be achieved as soon as possible. This grounds the baby with maximum physical contact. It is the initiation of the communications system of body-to-body, touch-to-touch (feeling-to-feeling), and the moment of first skin-to-skin contact is when and where grounding takes place.

Everything you have experienced to the point of sufficient neurological development is still there in your memory and serves as a source of pain or pleasure. If Mommy and Daddy see that their baby's needs are met on a consistent and child-centered basis, that baby will become what we call psychologically superior. Baby will have a significant, profound, and deep belief in its right to exist in this world. With a place in the sun, with people seen as primary sources of pleasure, identity is available. If people aren't sources of pleasure, the baby will pull away from the reality of people into the world of inanimate objects and intangible activity—eating, drinking, and often excessive consumerism.

Everyone needs strokes—negative or positive, kisses or kicks—in order to satisfy their stimulation stroke hunger. When Mommy and Daddy engage in a conversation that attempts to elicit negative, gamey strokes, they are gratifying their stroke hunger. Their actions speak to the fact that they were taught this way as children, and now they are passing the same system on to their child.

In order to talk straight, Mommy and Daddy must first learn that being critical of each other indicates a lack of unconditional accepting love of themselves first, and each other second. We give to each other what we give to ourselves. Therefore, it is important to love ourselves and then share that love with others through good, straight communication.

In this dialogue between pregnant mother and soon-to-be father, a loving communication would have been as follows:

Conversation:

Expectant mom: Honey, I want to talk to you about how I feel being pregnant. Are you willing to talk now or later?

Expectant dad: It's fine now. (*or*) We can talk later.

Expectant mom: I accept my responsibility for mistakenly believing I was protected from pregnancy. I also know that you did not intend to cause me pain by getting me pregnant. However, I really feel negative at this time and want us to talk from time to time about my feelings, so we can deal with them positively. I want to feel good and I want my baby to feel wanted. Are you willing to share my feelings?

Expectant dad: Honey, I know we goofed in getting you pregnant at this time, but I do want you and the baby to feel good, because I care about you both. I am willing to talk from time to time about your negative feelings. If I don't want to talk, I'll tell you straight. I don't want to play games with you. I love you.

With this kind of communication, both Mother and Dad are expressing their feelings and handling them appropriately. Baby benefits by having a nurturing mother's body in which to live, thus promoting good chemical communication between them.

26

BABY TALK

From the age of 7 months in utero, a baby is responding to pain and pleasure signals from mom's body. A wonderful scientific discovery in the last few years is that the negative anxiety producing cortisol does not cross the placental barrier, thus saving the fetus when mom is anxious.

If babies do not get stroked physically and emotionally, their mirror neurons do not allow bonding intimacy between the baby and the people who love them resulting in stroke deprived brain damage in the first three years of life. A baby must hear people speaking by ten months to replicate the sounds. Ninety percent of strokes are non-verbal such as tones of voice, gestures, postures, and facial expressions. How you speak emotionally is more important than the words under the age of three.

A baby's nervous system is modified with pain or pleasure. No strokes of any kind is worse than pain strokes and the result is a norepinephrine addiction to pain.

Baby: *Waaaauuuuuggghh!!*
Mother (to friend): Oh, she's spoiled. She always cries like that at this time. I let her cry it out. It's good for her lungs.
Baby: (Cries more, eventually crying himself or herself to sleep, or baby gets a spanking and then cries himself or herself to sleep.)
Mother: See I told you she would stop.
Rape!

Rape Analysis

Baby and Mom have participated in conversational rape. Baby is crying in order to seduce Mom into stroking her. Mom withholds the strokes, intimidating the baby to give up and go to sleep without strokes. Further, if the child is one, two, or three years old, Mother may even go in and spank the child, unfortunately enhancing a negative stroke system, and reinforcing for both an overall negative stroke economy. "She's spoiled." Mom's statement discounts the child as not being okay.

"She's spoiled" is a critical, non-nurturing, non-loving, ultimately negative rape message. If she were really a generous mother, she would say, "She may be okay. She always cries like that. And when she does, I respond to her." Mother love, which may be physical and/or mental, is unconditional.

The age-old rocking motion involved in mothering is very important for the baby. In effect, the rocking motion causes vestibular stimulation for the child. Neurological response, and hence neurological development—one of the last stages of the baby's development (mirror neuron stimulation)—is maximized. A caring and consistent mother who rocks, holds, and carries her baby, thereby insuring a neurologically well-grounded infant, is helping to guarantee her child a life with fewer physical, mental, and emotional problems.

In support of these thoughts, researchers indicate that our hunger for touch is absolute. Further, researchers actually quantify touch hunger with the simple identifying quotient that well-touched people are satisfied human beings. Infants in contact with their mother's body through the strapping or holding stages become pleasure-centered adults who know how to stroke both themselves and other people positively.

The first three months of the child's life, before either symbolic imagery or abstract cognition takes place, are especially important in this mother-infant contact. The goal is for the baby to have a good people-stroke economy, the result of fulfilling the touch hunger quotient.

Here is another scene between parents and a young child, now three years old. It is bedtime and the child is playing:

Mother: It's time to go to bed now.
Child (fussing): I want to play some more.
Mother: No, I said now! Do you want Daddy to spank you?
Child: *Waaaauuuuuggghh!!*
Mother: Okay, just a little longer.
Rape!

Rape Analysis

In this case, mother, baby, and the mentioned father indicate rape. Baby is learning to distrust people, leading to a loss of security. Inconsistent parenting and the loss of security leads to instability. The lack of trust is also a source of information about pain rather than pleasure.

Mother exercises rape, exhibiting a lack of security in herself to be a stable, giving person. She doesn't trust her own thinking, indicating a past rape of her own thinking process. In turn, mother passes the rape to the father, setting him up as the "Bogeyman" in the child's life, the bearer of pain.

If Dad accedes to Mom and spanks the child on her say-so, he is allowing himself to be raped through emotional intimidation. If he does not cause the child pain, Dad will receive pain from Mother (wife).

By the age of three, the baby has become cognitive, aware of symbolism. Mother's face is a symbol of pleasure. Going to bed is an awareness of loss of pleasure. Baby has become aware of the thought processes, including a memory, indicating that some actions are pleasurable and some are painful.

Pain and pleasure are both normal and natural concepts. They are feelings, and as such, nonnegotiable. Feelings exist, period; they are neither good nor bad. It is the exercise of those feelings, what you do with them, that counts. What you do with your feelings shows whether you are a rational or an emotional person.

Rational people have been taught early on that "Yes, pain exists." However, the teaching they received incorporated the stable advice that effective use of the brain will allow an appropriate action to be taken. Naturally, a baby goes toward pleasure and away from pain. Bed is painful; playing is pleasurable. Since Mother and Father are pain addicts (i.e., they are either habituated to pain or afraid of pain themselves), they allow the baby to dominate the home for the sake of gratification. The baby is being spoiled, developing an inability to deal with pain.

Mother shows her fear of pain. She doesn't want to anger the child, probably because she's afraid of the pain the baby will bring her. She feels insecure in facing that pain, so she avoids it and passes it on to Dad. In effect however, her transfer unreasonably gratifies her baby's pleasure want;

doing so, she sets no price on the behavior herself. The growing child is left without encouragement toward self-discipline.

The child learns or becomes aware that under all conditions, we have to have pleasure. Pain to the child is seen as destructive and negative. Pain is bad. Painful experiences are bad. The discipline of mother is lacking, because she fears causing pain. She is setting up a system of conditional loving, i.e., "If you do this, then I will love you," or "If you do that, I will not love you." In this case, Mother is saying, "If you don't cry or fuss, I'll love you."

The child, a victim of inconsistent parenting, naturally starts to set up a system. "Mother lets me stay up. Therefore, Mother loves me." The opposite of that is "Father makes me go to bed. Father requires me to perform. Father does not pay attention to my feelings. Therefore, Father doesn't love me."

The child learns to establish a full system of no-pain. These parents, also wishing a no-pain environment, stress performance at the expense of feeling. The singular process of pleasure has taken precedence over the balance of all feelings maintained in a pleasure-centered way. Without this balance, an uneven ratio develops, foundations for harmful systems are laid, and problems result in later life.

On the opposite extreme, what if the big, adult-sized members of the family were raised in an emotional way themselves? What if these adults were raised to feel their feelings and react spontaneously to their feelings, thinking only later of the results? This ill-balanced pattern adds up to chaos, and the child loses faith in people as a source of true information.

As a result, the child learns to pull away from human beings and gravitates toward trustable objects. Very often, these trustable objects might be totally invested in a world beyond reality, a world of daydreaming, fantasy, and imaginary people.

It is not inconceivable to state, then, that children we call "brains" have developed an addiction to books as a source of strokes. The books are object strokes, because the brainy child has lost faith in human beings. These children may be brighter than other people around them, or they may be unable to obtain positive strokes from their families.

If children under five years old are raised in a totally emotional, spontaneous way, the ultimate price tag will be what I call a pain-centered personality. The child refuses to seek pleasure, because pleasure is a no-no in the family. These children only perform. They only work. Life is for trudging. They become the game players of the world, or they become the total process-centered person who believes life is to be lived spontaneously—never mind what your head says the price will be.

Spontaneity produces chaos. Self-discipline allows for spontaneity. Mother and Father are models of self-discipline. Self-discipline means, "I feel my feelings. I think my thoughts, and I act on them rationally."

Straight Talk

What would be the straight talk in these situations? In the first case, if Mother wants to be a balanced nurturing mother, she will decide what performances are best suited for the ultimate good of the baby. She will, in a nurturing way, see that those performances are done, while taking into account baby's feelings or processes. Mother might find loving ways to negotiate with the young child.

A suggestion is "I'll rock you for a little while, and then you'll go to bed." Or take an inanimate object—a timer is a particularly good one—and say to the baby, "I'll set the timer, and when the timer goes off, then you will go to bed." Be sure to set the timer!

There are also loving suggestions that have existed for thousands and thousands of years, such as "Mother will read/tell you a story before you go to bed" and "Mother will sing to you before you go to bed." The performance of your actions or words should be that of a loving person. Feelings are tended, thinking is encouraged, and the consequent behavior takes into account both feelings and thinking.

With our older, more aware three-year-old, a straight talk, go-to-bed dialogue might be as follows:

Rational Conversation:
Mother: It's time to go to bed now.
Child: No! I want to play some more.
Mother: I know it's fun to play, and I will set the timer so you can play a little longer. (Timers are impartial.) When it goes off, I want you to go to bed without crying. Will you do that?

Child: Yes. (Or, "No." If no, then Mother elicits more talk until the child understands and agrees.)

If necessary, Mother promises a "prize" for performing, which may be a promise of quality together time when the child wakes up. Or, Mother may set a price tag on resistance, such as taking away a privilege, like TV, a bike ride, or a visit to grandparents.

Either way, the child is being instructed in how to integrate and process feelings and thinking with his/her acting performance. Mother is also demonstrating her abilities to integrate her feelings, thoughts, and actions as a role model for the child. Furthermore, Mother is showing her willingness to be a human being who can negotiate. She is encouraging the child to develop his/her own thinking, decision-making processes.

27

CHILDREN SHOULD BE SEEN AND NOT HEARD—THE GRADE-SCHOOL-AGED CHILD

In the first three years of life, children must experience trustworthiness with the people they experience. They must also feel safe enough to explore their environment, or they will labeled as loners and anti-social deviants. There are three main sources of strokes, people, places and things.

People can be pleasurable or painful. Pleasurable is based on negotiating skills, not intimidating with fear or seducing with guilt. A child under three must not be raised with intimidating fear or doubt and shame of self. Late teen or adult criminal behavior can be the result of lack of negotiating under three.

Conversation
Child: (Grade-school age, presenting an average report-card)
Mom/Dad: (By word or behavior) You could have done better.
Child: (Sad) I did my best.
Mom/Dad: That's not good enough.
Rape!

Rape Analysis

Where is the rape in this case? The dialogue exhibits parents who have themselves been raised in a performance-centered home. Their own parents' wishes were more important than their comfort. This system of performance over process is now important to them as parents.

These parents not only view thinking as more important than feeling but also see the actual behavior as more important than feeling good.

These parents were raped as children and now do the same to their own child. In this example dialogue, the child is convinced that he/she has done the best that can be expected. The parents are essentially replying in discount, saying: "That's not good enough. We're okay. We did it for our parents. Since you're not doing it for us, you're not okay."

Straight Talk

What would be a more appropriate exchange between parents and child? First, prior to analysis of the report card, parents need to take into account what they know about the child's academic capability. Is the child slow, average, or bright? After acknowledging the child's capability, those parents who want to motivate the child toward better performance may use the prize system.

The prize is not exactly a bribe; it is an appropriate form of motivation. If a paycheck can be considered bribery, our lives are spent giving and taking bribes. However, the lack of it leaves us in a deprived state. Simply stated, we are rewarded for our efforts throughout our lifetimes. Certainly then, parents who want to promote performance will do well to reward; they will do well to give prizes to their children for appropriate behavior.

Are the parents in the position to operate such a reward system? Are they able to feel self-stroked, so that they are not living vicariously through the child? Are the parents comfortable with their own lives, their own systems? If these parents are able to feel good about themselves, then they are what I call *peer parents*, parents who avoid playing one up and one down with each other.

Peer parents negotiate with their children based on the tangible reward. For some parents, notions of prices and prizes conjure up some mystical malevolence. These are the parents who insist to the child, "I want you to do so because I say so." In effect, these parents are putting egoistic pressure on children to be altruistic. These parents see the peer parent statement, "I want you to do so, because this or that will happen," as being in control—i.e., bad! Prices and prizes are seen as being unmeaningful.

Is this truly the case in life? Certainly when we're little we tend to want our strokes to come in concrete, observable, sensuous, situation-response ways—candy, prizes, or goodies. As we mature, we still want strokes, though a simple pat on the head or a verbal affirmation may fill the bill.

There is a false pride on the part of parents who point to the maturity of their children, exhibited by a child's obedient response to the simple statement: "I want you to do it."

In point of fact, "I want you to do it," means *you should do it.* Performance is taking precedence over process. Think about that statement, the parent telling the child, "I want you to do it." Behind this ostensibly mature instruction is the following kind of thinking: *I don't care that you feel intimidated. I don't care that I am motivating you through fear of being either rejected or abandoned by me. In fact, I'm going to convince Grandma and Grandpa and everyone in the neighborhood that you did it because you are such a good kid.*

To this, add: "No one will ever know that what I've done is totally intimidate and rape you into doing it, that there has been no negotiation. I wanted you to do it, and you did it, period."

These families that suppress the expression of wants in favor of performance *shoulds,* may, on the surface, be heralded as polite. However, the extremely polite child grows up facing an impotence in determining his or her own wants. Do they know what they want, where they want to go, what they want to do, and how they want to do it? The child, in pleasing the I-want-you-to-do-it parent, is rewarded from birth through age eighteen. From eighteen onward, however, he or she is punished through lack of self-gratifying reward and will often need extensive therapy.

Politeness is important but inappropriate when it is an outgrowth of a family that practices intimidation-rape. The response of the child is, "I'll do it your way, because you know more about it." In effect, surface politeness is seen and consequently rewarded. However, *should* is being stressed over *want.*

Peer parents know that children are children and that, mercifully, good children strokes need only be simple prizes or very simple concrete prices. This system does not lead to the spoiled child. Spoiled means the child receives everything he or she wants, because the child or parent is incapable of dealing with the element of pain. The child must have the human right to negotiate with the parents. The child must be able to state what he or she wants.

But the very act of negotiation equates with the fact that the child may or may not get what he or she wants. The child is not spoiled when pain is seen simply as an element/feeling with which he or she must deal.

The major premise of this book is that the language we use indicates how okay we are. The parental language trainer conversationally rapes the child by saying, "You should do it because I say so. Parents are more important than kids." The beginning of a conversational rape has commenced coincidentally with the beginning of language training.

Very quickly after birth, babies begin to convert their pure feelings of pain and pleasure into symbols representing these thoughts and feelings. By the age of one to two, they have picked up words and meanings that label their thoughts and feelings.

Those people who are responsible for teaching these words and meanings to the young child in effect control the child's communication skills within and outside the child's head. The impact of this control is far-reaching.

If the adult in charge is himself a seducer or intimidator, then he or she will have an adverse effect on the child's psychological development in several ways. The child may be led to believe that he or she is on earth to please others.

Or, the child is made to feel guilty when not pleasing others before self. Worst of all, the intimidation of the young child through harsh or critical language training convinces the child that obedience to authority is the goal of life.

Examples of other words and phrases that the seductive and/or intimidating parental language trainer uses in conversational rape are as follows:

"Say 'May I?' or 'Can I'? instead of 'I want,' or 'No.'"

Parents often mandate that a child "Be polite and say 'I wish,' or 'Would it be all right?' or 'Could we please do it?' rather than express his or her requests in a straightforward statement of 'I want,' or 'I do not want.'" But couching one's desires in polite or politically correct phrasing actually undermines one's personal worth and self-esteem. The child will grow into an adult who thinks it is unacceptable to express his or her desires without sidestepping into some type of verbal intimidation or seduction to soften the request. But the person who can freely say, "I want" and "I do not want," even when it causes others some conflict or pain, is someone who will not be intimidated or seduced into a pattern of conversational rape situations later on in life.

"Tell people you're sorry for your mistakes."

A child who is intimidated or seduced into apologizing for mistakes is really being trained to curtail experimentation. But when exploration and creativity are shut out of the child's personality, the result is stagnation. All potential learning activities are seen to promote mistakes, and the child has been trained to feel guilty about making mistakes. The better way is to assist the child in accepting mistakes as a necessary part of learning in life. The most important lessons we learn in life are the lessons we learn from our mistakes.

"Tell me why you think or feel or do things."

Here, the language trainer is saying, in effect, "Prove to me who you are, and only then I will accept you." Since there is no way to prove a *why*, children eventually lose confidence in both who they are and the validity of their own thoughts and feelings. Demanding *why* insists the child produce empirical proof, i.e. something the questioner can see, taste, touch or hear, which is an impossible burden when dealing with subjective matters.

But when you ask a child "What are your reasons?" it only requires the child to provide basic data about a subjective experience, a straightforward statement of feelings or emotions. The parent can then use this as a basis to examine alternative actions resulting from these feelings and analyze the costs of such actions. Remember, feelings themselves cannot be negotiated; they exist in and of themselves.

But you can present an objective price-prize case to children that certain actions taken in response to their subjective feelings have resultant consequences in the world that they should become aware of. They can then learn to make rational choices of how they choose to express natural feelings.

"You need me. I am your provider and protector, your trainer."

The child who is taught to need certain people, places, or things becomes a needy adult. All humans have certain basic physiological needs. They need food, water, air, and shelter to stay alive. They need strokes or stimulation mentally and physically—either positive pleasure strokes or negative pain strokes—to remain psychologically comfortable. They need a nervous system to record experiences taken in through the five senses of taste, touch, smell, sight, and hearing.

They need an education to achieve strokes for their mind and body as well as training in how to structure their time on short- and long-term bases. But overuse or misuse of the word —"I need to get a new dress," "I need a certain person, a certain thing, a certain place to be okay"— is a seduction and/or intimidation of the child into overemphasis of those people, things, or places. This is conversational rape that undermines their flexible, creative, spontaneous, and autonomous way of seeing themselves, others, and life in general.

Our Branding in the "OK Corral"

Each one of us holds a basic attitude about life, our life position that we learned from our language trainers before we were five years old. This is a very subjective view of where we stand in relationship to other people in our lives. Three examples of this attitude reflected in life are as follows:

If we were intimidated by harsh or critical, controlling people, our life position will probably be, "I'm not okay unless I earn your conditional love. You are more okay than I am."

Another not-okay position is produced by the overlooking, overgiving, seductive super-parent who seduces the young child into feeling guilty for asserting himself or herself or contradicting the parent. This child will also carry away a life position of "I'm not okay because I continue to want things," or "Say no for me," or "I should take care of your needs, not mine." Some churches are also very into promoting this "others first, me second" guilt.

The worst rape of all is the one produced in the drug- or alcoholic-violent home where even a young child knows that the parents are not okay. Out of need and love, however, the child will unconditionally accept a position of, "My parents are not okay, and neither am I." This child now has incorporated the type of self-defeating attitude that will later lead to becoming the same type of self-destructor for his or her children.

Gender Differences

Now, let's view a typical situation involving the parents' reaction to a child's level of success in school. It may be politically incorrect to point this out, but there are psychological as well as physical differences between boys and girls. These gender differences necessitate a different parental reaction in each case.

When a little girl brings home a report card and cries that she didn't get all the As and Bs that she thinks everybody wanted her to get, Mommy and Daddy are earnest in providing a balance of feeling and process. Daddy would say, "I really do understand you feel bad about your report card, dear, and I think it would be a good idea if you sat down for fifteen minutes every night after supper and went over your math and spelling. How do you feel about this? What can we do to help you feel better? Do you want to stay after school with your teacher? What do you think would be a good system?"

If it's a little boy coming home and crying about the same situation, Mother can say to him, "Son, I do appreciate your situation, but I want to hear what your plans are for improving. And when you know what your plans are, I want you to let us know, so that your father and I can assist you in carrying them out." After working out a plan of action together, Mother and Dad can then talk to him about his feelings and nurture him generously.

So in essence, stress is placed on the daughter's feelings, primarily, and then the solution is worked out. With the son, the solution is worked on primarily. Attendance to his feelings is secondary. You cherish a girl's feelings but respect a boy's abilities to think and problem-solve.

This approach also creates a very good prize because a system is established wherein attention is given to her feelings. She is rewarded, she is stroked, and her performance consequently improves.

To the little boy, the parent says, "How do you plan to solve this problem? I want to know what your solution is." The little boy straightens up and says, "Dad, I want to … um … I want you to sit down with me after supper and help me with my school work, so I can get better. Will you do that?"

Dad's response is straightforward and reinforces his son's masculinity. "That sounds like a good idea, son."

In each case, you've achieved exactly the same results—to sit down for quiet study after dinner. Then, during the study time, Dad and son can talk about their feelings, whether positive or negative, in order to share and bond.

But, in obtaining these exact same results, what was the principle difference?

With the little girl, there was some assistance and some support system underlying reason, but primary attention was given to her feelings; i.e., her sadness, her frustration, her reaction to the bad report card. With the little boy, the feelings were acknowledged, but because he was facing some stress in solving his problem, the parent acted as a coach: "How are you going to solve this, son?"

If the boy came up with, "I don't know. I don't know how to solve it," the parents would have continued with proper encouragement by saying, "Well, we want you to think of a solution, and we want you to recognize what that solution is." The boy, importantly, was not discouraged into playing dumb. Rather, he was motivated to solve his problems, and only afterward was consideration for his feelings offered.

On the other hand, the parents first responded to the girl's feelings, then rewarded her, and only when she was feeling better did they assist her in solving her problems.

In families where little girls are raped conversationally and are promoted to act as "little boys," too often the girl will hold her feelings in. As a result, she really can't solve her problems. Suppressing her feelings, she may offer, "I'm going to stay after school," but many times her bad feelings will lead her to decide, "I'm not going to do anything at all." She becomes either rebellious and resistant or submissive and shy. Very often, a little girl tends either to overperform in a bid to win objective approval from parents who do not encourage her to share her feelings, or she winds up feeling so bad she gives up all such attempts, and under-performs— without sharing her feelings with her parents.

It works exactly the opposite with boys. Little boys very often over-express their feelings. Mommy's boys, initially emotional, receive immediate attention to their feelings, and then somebody even comes in and solves their problems as well. These children eventually grow into young men who learn to employ this process in all their relationships; they yo-yo their feelings in overuse and underuse, manipulating responses from people around them.

Little boys who get the idea that the way to solve any problem is to become emotional are in effect learning to use female manipulation tactics. This will not serve them well in the competitive world they will face as grown men.

Similarly, little girls who become so overwhelmed by their feelings, whether overdoing or underdoing in their reactions to their feelings, will face trouble later on in life. They become an over-do-it parent-mother who gets overstressed by the demands she places on herself, which negatively affects her health, or she will morph into a helpless Daisy-Daffodil type of woman, unable to operate without constant human catering. The men in their lives experience them as high-maintenance women and very often will ultimately bail out of any relationship, seeing it as too expensive.

Let's conclude by talking for a moment about the parents' role in fostering a child's sexuality.

A significant impact of the report card scenario we have just discussed is that boys and girls learn not just their self-awareness and self-esteem through language training but also they develop their lifetime sex-role identity. Parents need to be aware of the importance of their cross-gender roles.

Father is more important as a trainer for his daughter than mother is. Father assures his daughter of her sexuality: "You are a woman," or "You are going to be a woman." Mother reinforces the message by telling her, "I'll show you how to do it."

In contrast, Mother assures her son, "You are a boy, and you will grow up to be a man, and your father is going to show you how to do it." And father will act as the boy's principle male role model.

Our sexual identity is learned from the opposite-sex parent, but we unconsciously model after the same-sex parent. The confusion a child experiences with either transient, nonexistent, or multiple parent figures is therefore easily understood. The confusion is underscored as the child must decide in this early childhood period which heroes and heroines to identify with.

The significance of language training cannot be overemphasized. Anyone in a position to provide language training to young children would benefit both themselves and their trainees through exploring therapy programs, including my own program of Androgynous Semantic Realignment™, WANT ® Training.

28

RESPECT YOUR ELDERS—
THE TEEN YEARS

Nature is a second source of strokes physically and emotionally. Water, sand, grass, rocks, threes, and animals can be very healing for children from 3-12 years old, especially in a family or loving group.

Last, but seriously dangerous are things: drugs, casual sex, eating and money. Between the ages of 13-18 nature lowers dopamine production in boys and girls which leads them out of the family nest into the world of gangs and lower family controls if unattended.

Conversation:
Teenager: Do I look good for my date tonight?
Daddy: Get that lipstick off! Do you want people to think you're a bad girl?
Teenager: Please, Dad, all the girls wear it.
Daddy: I don't care. No daughter of mine is going out looking like a tramp. *Rape!*

Rape Analysis

The girl has been conversationally raped of her recognition as a girl in her father's eyes. It is very, very common for fathers who feel significantly threatened by their teenage daughters' sexuality. They experience guilt about their sexual attachment to their daughters, not realizing this is an absolutely normal occurrence.

As we wrote earlier, the male parent's role is to reassure his daughter of her sexuality and help her to grow into a properly sexualized woman.

Handled well, the natural sexual attachment of a father enhances the girl's self-esteem as a sexual human being.

But if he feels threatened by the daughter's sexuality, the father can fear she will become aware of his response to her and expose him as a "dirty old man." As a result, he will very often discount her feelings as a maturing female and attack her in matters of clothing and make-up, areas of great significance in the teen years.

If you will recall, the feelings of the body are directly connected to the mind and thinking, and they result in action. Little girls are primarily feel-thinkers, while little boys are primarily think-feelers. So when a girl's feelings, especially those she has about her femininity, are attacked or go unsupported, she is significantly castrated as a desirable woman.

A father's discounting of his daughter's emerging sexuality vis-à-vis her use of lipstick is in effect a rape of that marvelous support that only a father can give as the major male figure in a girl's life.

Ironically, the very fact that the father is attempting to deemphasize his daughter's sexuality can have the reverse effect of promoting it—but in a negative fashion. Rebellious actions such as sexual promiscuity often result significantly from a female not receiving support as a woman from the leading father figure in her life. She finds it extremely difficult to express her femininity appropriately and will very often become self-destructive.

This can find expression in both sexual promiscuity and, tragically, in the areas of overeating and alcoholism, both of which relate directly to body systems. Sadly, girls who are not secure about their femininity often sedate their feelings through the use of self-medication and addictive chemicals, such as sugar, drugs, or alcohol.

So what leads a father to conversationally rape his daughter? It's very likely that he was similarly raped himself earlier in his life when his mother figure was significant. A man is threatened by femininity either because of an inappropriate or nonexistent relationship with his own mother or the principle female in his life. When he does not feel secure in his own masculinity, his ability to respond is crippled. He cannot hang an identification factor on the male side of his role.

As a consequence, when he becomes a father such a man will not be able to convey masculine support to any female, and this is clearly demonstrated in his relationship with his daughter. Many little girls are Daddy's little girl up to puberty, at which point they are completely abandoned by their fathers. This abrupt rejection has a highly negative effect at a very critical time in their development as maturing women, and it impacts their feelings of self-worth as women throughout the rest of their lives.

Straight Talk

In talking straight, in terms of a girl and her father, it is helpful to refer to Carl Jung's theory of anima and animus, also demonstrated in the ancient Chinese concept of yin-yang energy balance. Every female has an animus element of masculinity, self-assertion, and aggressiveness. Every male has his anima: his sensitive, instinctive, responsive feminine aspect. If you will recall my earlier analysis, girls feel-think, with feeling comprising their feminine experience: sensitivity, warmth, and responsiveness.

If a father does not play the role of "Daddy" by cherishing her exterior feminine (or yin) side, then he will instead become a "father" by generally promoting her interior masculine (or yang) aspect. This results in a woman who cannot cherish her own feelings, a woman who is more into performance than she is into process—in short, an unfeminine woman. And she will have difficulty responding from her female side to any man later in life.

So what can a father do to become more of a "Daddy" and cherish his daughter's feelings? A man cherishes a woman's feelings by maximizing adjective verbiage. He tells her, "You're a *lovely* girl. You're a *loving* person. You're a *kind* person." Adjectives are cherishing statements. A father's use of them promotes his daughter's exterior femininity. This allows her to fully feel her body protected by her interior animus strength internally, without sacrificing her femininity externally.

When a woman wears her interior strength on the outside, as a form of protective armor, this costuming as a "man" can only be done at the loss of her feminine exterior. The secret of being a well-balanced woman, starting in her younger years, is to keep her internal strength strictly reserved to herself. To do this, though, she has to feel that her exterior is properly psychologically protected, and this can only be accomplished through the direct cherishing words and actions of a man toward her.

A woman *thinks* in self-preserving terms internally and gives in a generous way exteriorly. This is exactly opposite to the way a man perceives reality. A man gives in a generous way exteriorly, but *feels* within himself. He still has that female aspect within him called the anima, and when the man takes care of his feelings interiorly, he will generally perform in a self-preserving way.

There is one verbal error that many people make that I call the Pretty Girl Syndrome. Prettiness is mistakenly treated as a performance marker: "You look pretty. You dress very well. You do your make-up very well. You keep a good house." But such statements as these are non-adjectives. They are, rather, very performance-oriented strokes.

How can a man change his language into *cherishing* language? He would say, "You're a very *sensuous* woman. You are a very *attractive* woman." These are very nice things to say. A stroked performance is not as fulfilling to a woman as stroking her process of being a loving woman.

Basically, a man does better to stroke the magnetic feminine qualities. "You're loving, you're sweet. You're kind and sexy. You're attractive, giving, and you're very generous." Use these statements as opposed to "You *do* something very well."

A male stroke—a performance stroke—would be, "You cook a very good meal."

There is a difference when you say, "That was a very loving thing you did," or "That's a very generous thing you did—the love you show when you cook so well." This is a marvelous statement to make to your daughter.

Now, let's take another look at a possible dialogue between mother and son:

Conversation:
Son: Mom, I'm taking Sally to the prom.
Mother: No, dear, she's not our kind of people.
Son: But Mom, she's a neat girl and I like her.
Dad: Listen to your mother, son. She knows best about these things. *Rape!*

Rape Analysis

The first victim is the boy. His choices have been disrespected. Again, one of the primary jobs of a mother is to admire and respect her son's brains, because that's the part of him that will carry him forward as a man in the world of reality. So a mother says in effect, "Son, your brains aren't too cool. Mine are better than yours. I know what's best."

Now, in this case the mother has obviously been trained and raised to be a performer herself. She's evaluating the performance level of this "neat girl." Mother's performance orientation begs the question—what happened in her childhood? Likely, there was a father figure or lack of a father figure who promoted the overstressing of her animus decisional qualities over her instinctive creative qualities.

A mother perpetuating a need to be respected for her thinking more than needing to be cherished for her feelings will soon have this young man becoming more and more dependent on her problem-solving capabilities.

He will begin to ask, "Mother, should I? What do you think, Mother?" This will not allow him to identify with the male side of the role, and he will eventually become a female-trained man, a second-class operative in a society that still prizes the masculine markers of competition, conquering, and control.

Dad, on the other hand, relinquishes his own masculine authority by deferring to a woman's judgment instead of using his own man-to-man sharing ability and making his own case toward his son. This indicates that he no doubt deferred to his own mother and other strong women as a young man. Thus, his own rape shows up now in the way he now trains his son to similarly defer.

Supporting one another is a good thing for a mother and dad, but remaining individuals in their unique masculine and feminine roles is one of the significant gifts they each can give their children.

Straight Talk

How might this situation have been resolved more gender-appropriately? When the son announces, "Mom, I'm taking Sally to the prom," Mother might have said, "That's nice. What kind of girl is she?" Son would have replied, "She's a great girl, Mom, and I like her."

Mom then responds with a positive stroke: "I trust you to use your head, son."

If, on the other hand, Mother sensed something potentially inappropriate was developing, she might have suggested that her son invite this girl over, so that she might get to know her.

Mother's feelings are totally appropriate, in that she is being stimulated by her son's emerging sexuality. Once again, a mother and son are having a normal love affair. She is receiving a lot of her masculine strokes from her son, and he is receiving feminine strokes from her. By holding back an immediate expression of her fears and not using them to manipulate the boy's performance or to protect her own feelings, Mother gathers and restructures the situation into one in which she can gather data in her own time and space. She is both taking care of herself and also not castrating her son out of potential fear and inappropriate action.

It's paradoxical. When women use emotion to run their logic, they become illogical. While it's true that women think with their feelings, hopefully they run their feelings through their heads before reacting emotionally.

Men think through their mental logic, but hopefully they apply their logic with a sense of tenderness and sensitive feelings. Since a mother is the primary male trainer for her son, it is absolutely appropriate that her vocabulary employ many verbs. "You did that well, son. You're a very bright person. I really *admire* how you did that. I *respect* your choices. I *believe* you know how to do it. Good show, son." Hopefully, mother and father are the first "love affairs" their children will have. With good sexual communication, the parents will be successful as models for future true affairs.

One great device for giving everyone in the family a voice is the family game. Once a week, at a regular time, meet as a family for a council meeting. At these council meetings, each member, beginning with the oldest and ending with the youngest, brings up a want (yang) or a not-want (yin) for negotiation. Each person's requests are respected and a sincere effort made to build a compromise agreement that helps the family blend and build family goals, *us*, and traditions.

The oldest member present is the moderator, seeing to it that cross fighting is stopped and rules of order prevail:

Rules of order for a family council:

1) Be a gracious winner.
2) Admit when you are wrong.
3) Bring up one want or not-want at a time.
4) Agree to disagree this session. Bring it up next time.
5) No intimidation with threats or guilt seduction.
6) Be willing to apologize when you break these rules.
7) A win-win session is: you both feel good in your bodies.
8) You're not resentful or holding a grudge.
9) You are grateful for the council meeting.

Each member present (hopefully all members are present, as missing members may be the ones who cause the most trouble) is allowed to ask for one thing they want, or say no to one thing they don't want from any or all family members present.

Each issue is negotiated without intimidation or seduction games.

The issue must be specific, not general. "I don't want you, Mary, to take my clothes without first getting permission." Not, "Don't come into my room ever again!" You cannot negotiate abstracts like, "Be nice. Stop being mean to me." Only practical issues can be negotiated, such as "I want you to say hi when we meet at breakfast" or "I don't want you to hit my head with your finger." It must be something that can be tasted, touched, smelled, seen, or heard by the senses. Asking for love is general; asking for a hug is specific.

The family members go around until all members say, "Pass. I'm done."

This venting of issues regularly, with each person having an equal voice and only age, not power or favoritism, determining rank, will blend the family members into a loving communicating unit, *us.*

29

EXTENDED FAMILY AND FRIENDS— OLDER MEMBERS

This is my happiest chapter because I am in my 80's and loving my life. I've done it all - good and bad. I am, by giftedness, a musician (piano/organ) and a fine artist. I am not a solo musician, I was an accompanist for soloists, choirs, school singing groups and a good pastel artist.

I am forty four years sober off sugar and alcohol, married four times, buried three wonderful boyfriends, mother of four wonderful daughters who given me five grandsons, two granddaughters and two great granddaughters.

I have learned the secret of my life and I teach it whenever I can. To be happy, you must:

1. Love someone (or animal)
2. Have a purpose each day serving others
3. Look forward to something (bucket list)

Grandma/Grandpa: We'll babysit for you, honey.
Son Mark or Daughter Kathy: No, Mom and Dad, you just sit right down and enjoy your retirement … you've earned it.
Grandma/Grandpa (unspoken): But we don't want to sit around waiting to die. We want to be a part of the family.
Rape!

Rape Analysis

And so it is at the end of our lives in this country. By promoting dependency on the young or the government, we often condemn our senior citizens to a sentence of both sitting idle and waiting for death.

It can often appear as if we force elderly people back into filial symbiosis reminiscent of the original infant symbiosis. Once again, language and conversation can happily perpetuate autonomy, creativity, and spontaneity—or language can insidiously perpetuate rape through power play conversations.

In families where only the "useful" moneymakers participate in family decision-making, senior citizens lose the vote. They lose their voice when they lose their earning power. They are seen in human function as no more then babysitting sources or immediately available moneylenders, with no questions asked.

Sometimes the elderly are convinced to sell homes they love and move into ghetto retirement villages. Some, but certainly not all, of these retirement centers equate with preschool childcare establishments. Those that are poorly designed limit movement under a watchful eye; in a disguise of entertainment, institutional care is pushed.

Sometimes, when chronic medical problems exist that interfere with the social life of the family, Mom and Dad become a burden to be suffered from a distance. Medical and behavioral sciences talk about the need for body contact and intimacy for the young child. Ironically, the elderly person with the same problems is often neglected.

Possessive children sometimes refuse to support or encourage budding romances among the elderly. These children do so out of misguided visions of senior citizens as sexless and not in need of either relationships or the intimacy they can provide. Companionship at this time of life is an actual aid to longer life. In fact, mutual caring and sharing with another human being promotes physical, mental, and emotional health.

On the other side of the fence, there are elderly persons who take advantage of their "second childhood" and often revert to behavior classified as spoiled in children. Verbal demands, whines for attention, and willful, rejecting actions will surely promote conversational rape for all parties. The guilty or angry younger person resents being taken advantage of by the willful parent and often retaliates by rejecting and abandoning the parent in his or her twilight years.

Also, there is the phenomenon of the helpless Daisy and David

Daffodil elderly couple, which can totally disrupt the family life of a child by refusing to promote self-centered care and responsibility. It almost appears that the parents are seeking a payback for all the services rendered to the dependent son or daughter years earlier.

Straight Talk

In an appropriate and healthy relationship between senior and junior family members, there exists a conversational system that is founded on "I want" and "I do not want." Rape does not exist, because respect permeates the relationship. Whenever possible, situations are negotiated on equal terms. No one is one-up or one-down due to physical or mental standing. Love has become the watchword.

Children raised by rational, child-centered couples later become rational, loving parents to the couple who raised them. They end the cycle of life on the same theme—feelings and not-wants are to be cherished, and thoughts and wants are to be respected, by using the mind to design loving actions that promote self-love, respect, and esteem.

The purpose of life is to have the experience of living. The experience of living, in turn, is to seek pleasure and love for self and to share it with others. The only behavior that is totally learned, totally environmental, is the behavior of love. This is in contrast to given hereditary characteristics in the physical, mental, and emotional areas. We learn to love ourselves from our parents through language. We share this with others the same way.

When parents teach children to love themselves successfully, they are almost certain to guarantee a comfortable old age in which this loving lesson returns tenfold in loving concern and respect.

30

TO THINE OWN SELF BE TRUE

This last chapter is a continuation of my life statement in chapter 29. If you have benefited by this book, please pass it on.

"We don't stop playing because we grow old; we grow old because we stop playing." - George Bernard Shaw

Conversation:
Internal Critical Parent: You should have done it better, stupid.
Submissive Adaptive Inner Child: You're right; I should have done it better. I *am* stupid.
Rape!

Rape Analysis

As I have said previously, dealing with the conversational rape of children under five, poor language training, leads to an inhibition of the child's autonomy, creativity, and spontaneity.

Parents, schools, churches, and cultures often teach children, for example, that mistakes are wrong, or you must know before you do something that it is right, good, and proper—or don't risk doing it.

Such teachings are in error. You and I can be autonomous only if we believe that we will not be rejected or abandoned by those we love because we did something wrong.

Conditional love crushes creativity or spontaneity, because it mandates that we must follow *shoulds* that others deem appropriate, rather than *wants*, which we intuitively seek out of pleasure for ourselves.

Straight Talk

Once again, I'm going to make what will at first seem like a politically incorrect statement. But follow through on my logic.

Emotionally healthy people are self-centered people. Self-centered people often seem selfish, impolite, foolish, crazy, immoral, or downright illegal, because they are completely willing to follow their own inner spirit and to risk making mistakes. People who are selfless, however, are inherently unhealthy. Selfless people often seem generous, polite, logical, moral and legal—but it's because they compromise their integrity to fit themselves to the design of their surroundings. They do this by sacrificing their personal wants and embracing the security of the shoulds imposed on them from the outside by family, friends, and society in general.

From these propositions, we see that people come in two styles. They are either I-centered or they are question-mark (?) people.

I-centered people reason within themselves about the prices and prizes of possible actions. They do or do not do things depending upon what they personally will get out of an action they take. They never give or take things from other people over five years old unless they personally will benefit. By personally profiting from an action, they unconditionally accept or reject their gift. They have already received their internal prize of personal pleasure, self-esteem, self-love and self-respect.

Question-mark (?) people always do things for or against others because they react to shoulds from outside themselves. If they do something for someone, they assume and expect a reward. They have an overriding motto emblazoned across their coat of arms: "I do this for you, therefore you should pay me back." Their lives comprise an unending tally sheet, wherein they constantly check to see if they are in the black or in the red. And since they are usually in the red, they are constantly angry, because other people are perceived as not properly paying them back for all the generous gifts they have freely bestowed upon their vassals, without request.

Inside every generous Super Parent person hides a sad little Adapted Child, who was taught before age five that shoulds were better than wants as a medium through which to earn love and avoid rejection and abandonment.

Inside every intimidating Critical Parent person hides an angry, rebellious little Adapted Child who learned before age five that people are just plain mean and hurtful. They learned that the only way to avoid the pain of rejection and abandonment was to "get them before they get you."

Inside every Nurturing Parent person is a happy, curious, mischievous, brave little Fun Free child who goes after what he or she wants. They spontaneously pull away from what they don't want, because they learned before age five that love is never earned by good behavior. They learned that love is given freely because we exist in a world of sharing, caring people who themselves have learned that love is free.

When we talk to ourselves, we have two choices.

We can harass, criticize, dominate, intimidate, and conversationally rape ourselves like *they* taught us when we were little.

Or we can love ourselves unconditionally and share that love with others. We can nurture and accept ourselves and others, even when we make mistakes or they make mistakes.

I don't need to like or approve of other people.

I do need to love and accept or reject them but not tolerate them.

By talking straight to ourselves and others, we demonstrate unconditional loving acceptance and pleasure results. A sample, more loving dialogue, follows:

Rational Conversation:

Nurturing Parent Inside: You would have been better off doing it the other way, honey.

Fun-Free Child Inside: You're right, I would have been better off doing it the other way, and next time I'll do it that way. But I'm still okay, even when I make a mistake.

Made in United States
North Haven, CT
07 November 2021